Black Home Ownership

William A. Stacey

The Praeger Special Studies program—utilizing the most modern and efficient book production techniques and a selective worldwide distribution network—makes available to the academic, government, and business communities significant, timely research in U.S. and international economic, social, and political development.

Black Home Ownership
A Sociological Case Study of Metropolitan Jacksonville

PRAEGER SPECIAL STUDIES IN U.S. ECONOMIC AND SOCIAL DEVELOPMENT

Praeger Publishers   New York   Washington   London

PRAEGER PUBLISHERS
111 Fourth Avenue, New York, N.Y. 10003, U.S.A.
5, Cromwell Place, London S.W.7, England

Published in the United States of America in 1972
by Praeger Publishers, Inc.

Library of Congress Catalog Card Number: 73-186201

Printed in the United States of America

For Dorothy, Deborah, and William

This study is concerned with the social effects of housing on the individual and his normative orientation to society. The research established four major objectives: (1) to assess the social effects of housing and tenure on the individual's social adjustment by comparing a group of black Americans who were displaced and moved from the slum area to the status of homeowner in a newly developed suburb, to a group of black Americans that was displaced to adjacent slums retaining the status of renter; (2) to assess the relationship between social participation and social adjustment; (3) to assess the relationship between neighborhood satisfaction and social adjustment; and (4) to perform a multivariate analysis of the interrelationship between tenure, social participation, neighborhood satisfaction, and social adjustment.

The basic assumptions underlying this research are (1) Most individuals are goal-directed; however, their inability to achieve desirable goals or an uncertainty of suitable methods to use to achieve desired goals often causes problems of orientation for individuals in a specified social system. (2) In urban America, the slum areas of the city represent the end of the line for a large portion of the population; the crucial element here is that the inhabitants of slum areas feel this way about themselves. (3) A change from slum dwelling to suburban living results in a more positive orientation to society.

The major theoretical concepts used in this research were social adjustment, social participation, and neighborhood satisfaction. Social adjustment was assumed to be multidimensional. The dimensions delineated in this research were anomie, social isolation, and powerlessness. Scales were designed to measure the concepts.

The methodological procedure involved selecting a random sample of 458 from a population of 1700. The 1700 in the original population were black Americans who formerly lived in the most deteriorated section of a large southern metropolitan area. Chi-square was employed to analyze simple relationships. Coleman's attribute model was used to assess multivariate models.

The analysis of simple relationships indicates that tenure is significantly related to social adjustment, social participation, and neighborhood satisfaction. Both social participation and neighborhood satisfaction were found to be related to social adjustment.

The multivariate analysis revealed that tenure explained 20 percent of the variation in social adjustment, 12 percent of the variation in powerlessness, 7 percent of the variation in social isolation, and 5 percent of the variation in anomie. Social participation and neighborhood satisfaction did not explain as much variation as anticipated.

The findings led to the following conclusions: (1) The slums in metropolitan areas provide the background setting for producing alienated or socially unadjusted individuals. This is especially true for the black population. (2) A move from the slum areas to areas with better quality housing results in a more positive orientation to society. (3) If the move involves a change in tenure from renter to homeowner, a significant change in attitudes occurs. The feeling of powerlessness is significantly reduced. This is especially true for the black male. (4) Although not conclusively demonstrated, the change in tenure results in more frequent participation in community affairs and a greater satisfaction with one's neighborhood.

The findings and conclusions of this study were deemed to have theoretical, methodological, and pragmatic implications.

The successful pursuit of the sociological craft requires the student to view the discipline as a way of life instead of just a means to other ends. Specifically, for intellectual stimulation and bringing the author to accept this point of view, gratitude is owed Dr. Charles M. Grigg. The author also wishes to express his appreciation to other persons who contributed to this research, including Dr. K. Miller, Dr. T. S. Dietrich, F. R. Allen, and Dr. D. St. Angelo.

A special debt is owed Mrs. Marsha Peebles for her able assistance in editing the manuscript and Mrs. Susan Dickson for her patience and skill in typing several drafts of the manuscript. Larry Adrian, Jerry Fly, and William Howard are acknowledged for their assistance in reviewing the manuscript, computer processing, and statistical treatment of the data.

Special appreciation goes to my wife for her conscientious and painstaking efforts in typing the manuscript in its final form.

CONTENTS

APPENDIXES

LIST OF TABLES

Black Home Ownership

Housing has taken on a new meaning now that billions of dollars are spent annually in slum-clearance projects in almost all the major metropolitan areas of the United States. With the ever-increasing emphasis on urban development and on the consequences of poor housing conditions for a large portion of the nation's population, better housing has come to be viewed as a panacea for many of the social problems in American society.

Traditionally, descriptions and analyses of the problems related to the housing environment have been dominated by a concern for the physical aspects of the environment, such as hygiene and quantity of living space, and a concern in general for the social effects of slum dwellings. Merton has suggested that much of the early research in housing was virtually confined to a form of social bookkeeping.[1] He observed that

> during this phase, it was conventionally assumed that research comprised periodic audits of the proportion of the substandard dwellings, meticulously described in terms of defective structures, defective plumbing, and consequently, defective residents. . . . it was devoted to gross and uncritical correlations between slum areas with high frequency of substandard housing, a series of social morbidities; illiteracy, crime, juvenile delinquency, high mortality rates, poverty, public relief cases, illegitimacy and venereal disease.[2]

In more recent research, because of the belief that housing is a factor in the physical and social adjustment of the individual and family, the emphasis has been on the social effects of housing.[3] This more realistic perspective has arisen from the clinical and common-sense observations of physicians, public health officials, criminologists, law-enforcement agents, sociologists, welfare workers and others concerned with the health and social disabilities found in slum neighborhoods. Thus, studies have been designed to investigate the relationship between housing, health, and social adjustment. There is little doubt that such research efforts, directly or indirectly, may serve more theoretical ends by testing the validity of these commonly held beliefs and augmenting knowledge regarding the effects of slum dwellings on the normative orientation of individuals to society. [4]

In view of all the contemporary research that has been done on housing, there is one area of research that has received very little attention—forced displacement. [5] Relocation efforts resulting from urban renewal, slum clearance, and expressway construction, and their effects on the family and the individual must be assessed.

To many, relocation has become the symbol of inadequacy and frustration. It has meant the uprooting of families, enforced homelessness, sacrifice of neighborhood ties, threats to sources of political power, and equally important, the superimposing of a way of life quite often inconsistent with the very objective that such planning is intended to serve. [6]

Ideally, dislocated families should be given an opportunity to move from sites in accordance with well-defined development schedules that provide them with the maximum opportunity for better living and a minimum of social dislocation. [7] Thus, rehousing becomes the logical extension of public and social responsibility.

The present concern of the federal government for better housing has resulted from a series of emergencies: foreclosures and unemployment in the depression, housing for war workers, veterans' housing, and the general housing shortage after World War II. Consequently, the Housing Act of 1949 was passed.

> The general welfare and security of the nation and health
> and living standards of its people require housing devel-
> opment sufficient to remedy the serious housing shortage,
> the elimination of sub-standard and other inadequate hous-
> ing through the clearance of slums and blighted areas, and
> the goal of a decent home and a suitable living environ-
> ment for every American family. [8]

Since the passage of this act, several unanticipated problems—those concerned with relocation—have developed. Many slum residents have strong family and neighborhood ties in the slum community. Relocation tends to tear them away from their social roots and place them in a situation where new and painful social adjustments are needed. Second, relocation usually involves a movement to public housing, where families are placed in close proximity with others of similar economic status. This seems to be an unavoidable result of relocation, since the purpose of public housing is to provide homes for the poor and the displaced, and the criteria for obtaining it is specified formally in terms of need by the housing authority of the local municipality. Where forced movements have occurred, the displacement of families by governmental action frequently has produced anxiety or hostility, and consequently, a greater degree of alienation toward the community and governmental action, rather than stimulating greater participation in the "American way of life." The relocated population studied in this research experienced a unique departure from this pattern.

Because of the tremendous expense involved in rehousing, most communities have utilized federal funds in urban renewal programs and have typically resolved the problem by relocating the slum dweller in low-rent, federally sponsored housing projects. However, because of the stipulations of desegregated rehousing when using federal funds, and also because of the necessity of complying with the Housing Act of 1954, the community studied in this research utilized private sources to fund the rehousing of dislocatees. Thus, suburban housing developments in this community were constructed by private enterprise, and homes were made available to displaced families for a minimum down payment. Accordingly, nearly 66 percent of the slum dwellers moved from the status of renter in this southern metropolitan slum to the status of homeowner in a modern new suburb. It should be emphasized that relocation does not usually involve change in tenure. In the present instance, however, single units were made available to anyone who held a job, and the payment made on the house every month was in accordance with the resident's income. Thus, the individuals who moved to these new areas were given an unusual opportunity to change their tenure status from renter to homeowner.

Most of the traditional arguments for home ownership are of a qualitative social nature: security and independence, personal responsibility, family pride and status, civic participation, and so forth. All these arguments should be tested under the actual conditions surrounding home ownership today and implications that change in tenure have for the individual, the family, and society. Moreover, these questions are crucial in the rapid expansion of urban redevelopment programs. Do displaced families have strong neighborhood attachments? Are minority groups better or worse off after the move? Finally, what are the attitudes of black Americans who, though forcibly displaced by public action in a crowded city full of color barriers, are given an opportunity to experience one of the most important symbols of success as they move from being slum dwellers to homeowners in a modern housing development?

STATEMENT OF THE PROBLEM

The importance of housing is exemplified by a statement made
by Louis Wirth in the late 1940's:

> Housing is a social activity. . . . In housing, as in the
> study of other social phenomena, it may be well to start
> with the central social values involved. Hence, I would
> propose that the sociological study of housing begins with
> housing as a social value. Everyone in our society is
> concerned with the realization of this value, and the quest
> for achievement of this value by each affects the similar
> quest by all others. [9]

The changing status of the black American can be seen as
especially significant in the area of housing. Traditionally, the
black American, and other minority groups in general, have pre-
dominately occupied the most undesirable areas of communities.
This has most frequently, especially in the larger metropolitan areas,
been the slums. Furthermore, a major characteristic of the slum,
or rather the people living in this environment, is the fact that they
tend to be isolated from many of the activities and sentiments that are
necessary prerequisites for the integration of individuals into a dynamic,
mutually reinforcing social and economic system. Many slum dwellers
are isolated; some are alienated, which means they not only feel
separated from society, but also antagonistic toward society. [10]

Perhaps low economic status has been the major factor responsible for the minority groups' occupancy of slum dwellings. Because
of the low incomes of a large proportion of minority families, their
housing demand is mainly for the cheaper dwellings, which are found
most abundantly in the oldest and most deteriorated residential areas.
The residential history of Jacksonville adheres to this traditional
pattern.

Most recently, the economic position of the minority groups—
specifically black Americans—and consequently, their ability to com-
pete in the housing market, has improved. [11] As a result of population
increases in cities, and also of changes in urban social strata, available housing for black people has been generally adequate, both quan-
titatively and qualitatively.

With the housing legislation of 1949 and 1954 and the passage of
a subsidy bill in 1965, a number of low-income families have been
able to find more adequate housing. However, we must acknowledge
that many families in redeveloped areas are black, and this fact may

possibly reactivate any local patterns of prejudice and discrimination. [12]
As Boskoff points out:

> In practice, the search for adequate relocation areas be-
> comes studded with compromises. To be suitable, such
> areas should be within a reasonable distance from the
> central business district and from the sub-community in
> which displaced families previously lived. In addition, re-
> location areas should be relatively vacant, or marked by
> dispensable, intermittent land uses so that costs can be
> reduced. Finally, populations of adjacent areas must be
> willing to accept new housing developments for minorities.
> Several cities, among them Chicago and Atlanta, have de-
> layed in their relocation projects because of local opposi-
> tion and the sheer unavailability of land that satisfied rea-
> sonable planning conditions. [13]

The relocation project that is the focus of this study was necessitated
by the building of a new expressway that passed through the black ghetto of the city. This project was in some respects unique. An attempt
to upgrade the community in terms of moving out to better housing as
well as to provide the opportunity for the relocated people to change
their tenure from renter to homeowner was available. The change in
tenure and improved housing quality are two important focuses of this
research.

A preliminary report by Killian and Grigg indicates that housing
quality for all dislocatees was improved. [14] However the first phase
of this study will be to show that individuals changing their status from
renter to owner experienced a significantly greater increase in the
quality of the housing environment. Thus, for this research, improvement in the quality of the housing environment is a result of relocation.
In this case, relocation also resulted in change in tenure. It is noted
that relocation or change in tenure is not always followed by an improvement in the quality of the housing environment.

Of interest at this point is the manner in which quality of housing
was measured. Tangible indicators of housing quality such as amount
of privacy, amount of closet space, heating and cooling equipment,
street noises, amount of air and sunlight, open space around the house,
amount of room, and general satisfaction with the new residence are
used in the analysis.

A rational approach for the social scientist investigating problems
related to the housing environment is very difficult because of the
value system that has grown up around such problems. This is especially true in this research because the focus is on the change in tenure

and improvement in the quality of the housing environment. It is important to note that the ownership of a home is one of the most important symbols of success in American society. This idea has grown out of the ideas of utopia and sanitary reform movements in the nineteenth century. Even the phrase "home ownership" rather than "house ownership" is perhaps itself symptomatic of the aura of the sentiment that emanates from this particular form of property. [15] The idea of the urban reform movement was largely generated when housing density was correlated with the incidence of crimes of violence and with crimes against some form of property. Thus, the resultant social reform movements projected the standards of the middle class onto the program for the rehousing of the working class. [16]

Of particular relevance to this research problem is a recent statement by James Q. Wilson:

> As more affluent suburbs spring up, with neat lawns and good schools, the apparent gap between the quality of life in the central city and the periphery increases. The suburbanities, adjusting rapidly to residential comfort, become more discontented with the conditions that surround the places where they work in the central city, even though these conditions are also (on the average) improving. Those city dwellers who cannot, for reasons of income or race, move to the suburbs, grow increasingly envious of those who can; the prizes of wordly success are held up before their eyes but out of their reach. [17]

Since the displaced families studied in this research included the 34 percent who did not move to the suburb as homeowners, but who moved instead to adjacent slum areas, a test of Wilson's hypothesis is possible. Families moving to other slums would be expected to experience intensified social pathology from comparing their continuing frustration with the "success" of former friends and relatives living in their new middle-class suburb.

More important, perhaps, are the feelings of alienation of these families and their negativism toward society that results from their definition of the situation. Their definition is one in which the goal of home ownership was blocked by the local housing authority. After having perceived home ownership (a very important success symbol in American society) to be within their reach, they found, because of stipulations set forth by the housing authority, the opportunity to experience home ownership denied them. This situation provides the opportunity to test the D-M hypothesis. [18]

To illustrate more precisely the dimensions involved in this study, Frazier's study can serve as a specific example. Frazier has stressed the importance of economic factors and sociocultural conflict among the black Americans in urban areas. In the disorganized areas of Chicago, he found that the slum-dwelling black American family showed high proportions of broken homes, illegitimacy, and crimes of violence. However, among the black middle class and the stable working class, Frazier found the black Americans to be economically secure and to have adopted the normative patterns of the larger society.[19]

Many black Americans have not had the opportunity to acquire good quality housing.[20] For those who have had the opportunity to acquire good housing and, in this case, to become homeowners, it is important to assess the effects of housing quality and change in tenure on the social adjustment of the individual and the family.

This study, then, compares two groups of black American families in a large metropolitan area in the South. One group moved from renter status to the status of homeowner in the suburbs, while the other group moved from one slum area to an adjacent slum area. All families were displaced because of governmental action. The major focus of the study is on the following aspects of the influences of the home environment on the individual and society:

   1.   The relationship between change in tenure and housing quality

   2.   The relationship between change in tenure and social adjustment

   3.   The relationship between social participation and social adjustment

   4.   The relationship between neighborhood satisfaction and social adjustment

   5.   A multivariate analysis of the interrelationship between tenure, social participation, neighborhood satisfaction, and social adjustment.

Each general assumption is to be tested by a series of sub-hypotheses.

SIGNIFICANCE OF THE STUDY

In our affluent society, the homes of the poor are unsightly and in the way, and they arouse feelings that they must be demolished. Space must be made available for highways, office buildings, and

middle-income housing. Since 1949, nearly 700 cities have received
approval for almost 1,400 urban renewal projects. The magnitude
of this problem is further illustrated by the 66,000 families displaced
in the nation during the first ten years following the Housing Act of
1949. As a result of the increased pace of urban renewal in the United
States, the future national rate of involuntary displacement is estimated
at more than 150,000 families per year.[21] Thus, there is a practical
significance to the present study, because information is obtained on
the reactions to forced displacement. These reactions will be assessed
in the form of specific hypotheses discussed in a subsequent section of
this study.

Of equal importance, however, is the theoretical significance of
the present study. Rarely does one have the opportunity to empirically
assess one of the most frequently appearing conceptual schemes in the
study of disorganization. In this research, interest will be directed
toward studying the basic assumptions of Durkheim, Merton, and others,
and testing such assumptions to determine the correlates with social
adjustment. It is assumed by the author that forced displacement and
the influence of living in slum dwellings should be two decisive factors
in reinforcing and/or perpetuating feelings of hopelessness or despair.

In summary, the significance of the present study relates to two
basic objectives: (1) To assess the impact of forced displacement of
those black Americans who changed their tenure status from renter to
homeowner, as well as those families whose tenure status did not
change; and (2) to cast some light on the concept of social adjustment
when it is viewed as a multidimensional process, and in this way,
ascertain its implications for the social disorganization associated
with the housing environment.

PROCEDURES AND MAJOR DIVISIONS OF THE STUDY

Review of Relevant Literature

It is important to any scientific endeavor to be cognizant of
research that has been previously conducted in the same area or
similar areas of investigation. In the present study, it is necessary
to include a review of literature pertaining to the research on the
social effects of housing on the individual's attitudes and behavior as
well as to include the empirical researches relating these attitudes to
certain dimensions of social disorganization. Chapter 2 focuses on
the major themes that have pervaded the literature on slum dwelling
and social effects of housing environment on the individual and the
family. Attention is given to empirical research dealing with anomie
as a specific precedent to social disorganization.

Conceptual and Theoretical Perspective

Following from the literature review and drawing upon the understanding and interrelatedness of the factors considered in this study, Chapter 3 presents a basic conceptualization that, in effect, serves to develop theoretical propositions.

Methodological and Technical Strategy

Chapter 4 describes the sampling procedures employed in the present study, specific techniques of data collection, and construction of the instrument. Special attention is given to statistical techniques by which hypotheses are considered to be tenable or fallacious.

Analysis and Interpretation

Chapter 5 is an empirical assessment of the theoretical propositions presented in Chapter 3. In this chapter, data are examined and interpretations are advanced to account for the observed relationships. The data are then considered in terms of the broader theoretical perspective. Also, an attempt is made to verify, modify, and/or broaden the theoretical propositions advanced in Chapter 3. Limitations and implications for future research are included.

NOTES

1. Robert K. Merton, "The Social Psychology of Housing," in Current Trends in Social Psychology, ed. by Wayne Dennis (Pittsburgh: University of Pittsburgh Press, 1951), pp. 163-217.

2. Ibid., p. 163.

3. Daniel M. Wilner et al., The Housing Environment and Family Life (Baltimore: The Johns Hopkins Press, 1962).

4. Ibid.

5. This term came into the language at the end of World War II. It is descriptive of the physical urban renewal programs undertaken since then. The programs are sometimes called "Negro removal programs" or "slum dweller removal programs," since many residents of slums have had to move somewhere else to make room for new buildings. Thus, urban renewal has had the double objective of clearing slums and replacing them with better revenue-producing property such as business buildings or higher-rent apartment buildings. See David R. Hunter, The Slums: Challenge and Response (New York: The Free Press, 1964), p. 23.

6. Coleman Woodbury, ed., Urban Redevelopment: Problems and Practice (Chicago: University of Chicago Press, 1953).

7. Jack Meltzer, "Relocation of Families Displaced in Urban Redevelopment: Experience in Chicago," in Coleman Woodbury, ed., Urban Redevelopment: Problems and Practice (Chicago: University of Chicago Press, 1953), p. 407.

8. U.S., Statutes at Large, LXIII, Part 1, 413-45.

9. Louis Wirth, "Housing as a Field of Sociological Research," American Sociological Review, XII (April, 1947), 137-43.

10. Hunter, op. cit., p. 23.

11. Commission on Race and Housing, Where Shall We Live? (Berkeley: University of California Press, 1959).

12. Alvin Boskoff, The Sociology of Urban Regions (New York: Meredith Publishing Company, 1962).

13. Ibid., p. 335.

14. Charles M. Grigg, Lewis H. Killian, "Preliminary Report of Housing Survey, Jacksonville, Florida." Conducted July-October, 1962. Institute for Social Research, Florida State University, Tallahassee, Florida. April 10, 1963.

15. Merton, op. cit., p. 166.

16. Ibid.

17. James Q. Wilson, "The War on Cities," The Public Interest, III (Spring, 1966), 31-32.

18. The D-M hypothesis refers to the theoretical argument developed by Merton in Chapter IV of Social Theory and Social Structure (Glencoe, Ill.: The Free Press, 1957). A further elaboration on this proposition is presented in Chapter 3 of this book.

19. E. Franklin Frazier, The Negro Family in Chicago (Chicago: University of Chicago Press, 1932).

20. William McCord et al., Life Styles in the Black Ghetto (New York: W. W. Norton and Company, 1969), p. 28.

21. U.S. Senate, Subcommittee of the Committee on Banking and Currency, Study of Mortgage Credit, 86th Congress, 1st sess. (Washington, D.C.: U.S. Government Printing Office, 1959), p. 37.

2

INTRODUCTION

It has long been known that where housing is inadequate, major social problems exist. This can be demonstrated by pointing to the strong correlation between poor housing conditions and high rates of poverty, welfare cases, crime and delinquency, physical and mental health problems, and a large number of broken families. All evidence leads to the conclusion that one of the most important social problems that face urban America today, as well as in the foreseeable future, is providing good quality housing for all members of society.

According to public health papers, modern housing forms an extensive part of our human life:

> Healthful living conditions depend, to a large extent, upon the planning of the individual town or settlement. A dwelling is not merely a room or an apartment; it forms an integral part of the building, the street, and the town in which it is situated, well laid-out parks and gardens in residential areas should be regarded as important extensions of the individual dwellings."[1]

Beginning with the conceptual contributions of Marx and Engels, along with Durkheim, and continuing up to and including Merton, the reasoning suggests that it is in the areas where inadequate housing exists that one is likely to find the conditions that are detrimental to producing individuals with a positive orientation to society.

Accordingly, in September 1968, the Arkansas State Office of Health Planning established a task force to study the health of the family as related to its physical environment. They found that the underprivileged family is being forced to live with an inadequate quantity, as well as quality, of living space. It was noted that "a total of 602 persons living in 78 family dwellings occupy 305 rooms, for a ratio of two persons to each enclosed room of living space."[2] The extent of this crowding varies, but the negative effects are significant to one's physical and mental stability. Furthermore, these areas, frequently referred to as the slums, tend to trap people in a way of life that eventually results in feelings of alienation toward society. If these assumptions are valid, the slum represents one of the greatest dangers to American society. Hence, it is necessary to evaluate all possible alternative solutions to the problem. This research evaluates one possible, somewhat unique, solution to the "slum problem."

Although previous research has not established a causal link between the quality of housing that individuals occupy and specific factors leading to social disorganization, a number of relationships have been identified. The conclusions of several studies reviewed indicate that the slums represent a way of life and a way of looking at the future or, perhaps, looking away from it. This generalization suggests that it is necessary to focus on the factors responsible for originating and perpetuating these feelings. This necessity, in turn, means that research must concentrate on the attitudes indicative of social isolation and alienation in urban America. It is assumed that many of the primary factors associated with these feelings of despair originate in a deprived housing environment. Thus, for research concerned with the social effects of housing on human behavior to be productive, attention must be focused on individuals who have experienced a change in the quality of housing environment, and the effects of this change must be evaluated.

Further research efforts, which are also described in this chapter, have attempted to evaluate the change in attitudes and behavior of individuals associated with movement from slum areas to housing projects and other tenementlike dwellings. Findings indicate that certain positive changes are related to the change in residence. Positive findings, however, are counterbalanced by other research that indicates that the slums are merely transplanted from one area of the city to another. One may well be alarmed by the fact that almost no research has focused specifically on the relationship existing between relocation and change in tenure status.

Since this research is concerned primarily with the relationship between the quality of housing environment and indicators of social disorganization, it is necessary to evaluate some of the more significant previous research findings. According to a paper delivered to a seminar on housing and the environment, organized by the Conservative Party's Parliamentary Housing Committee, environmental flexibility should be the main objective in designing a housing project.[3]

This project focuses on the social and economic needs as well as the aspirations of the people. Moreover, it is from this focal point that Americans will inevitably assess the quality of the housing project, as compared to the cost of the project. As a result, the review will focus on two major themes: (1) The social effects of housing; and (2) home ownership.

SOCIAL EFFECTS OF HOUSING

There are several factors affecting variously the direction and content of the research and theoretical formulations concerning the social institution of housing. As early as 1951, Merton pointed to two basic social facts: (1) The social institution of housing is under-going important changes; and (2) housing involves the economic interests and social sentiments of all groups in American society.[4] Much later, it was also concluded by Wilner that the accelerating rate at which housing studies have been performed during the past thirty years in-dicates the humanitarian and pragmatic beliefs that housing plays an important part in health and social adjustment.[5] These statements illustrate the relative importance housing research has assumed and provide a basis for continuing the search for solutions to the social pathology associated with a deprived housing environment.

The early focus on the relationship between inadequate housing and social pathology resulted in housing legislation brought about the the depression, housing shortages, and other socioeconomic reasons. Commenting on this issue, Catherine Bauer states:

> The implicit purpose of all housing legislation is to pro-
> mote the general welfare, whether in terms of physical
> health, social and civic efficiency, national defense, pro-
> tection of the family, maintenance of business property
> and full employment, or the fulfillment of such social
> ideals as "equal opportunity" and "equal rights."[6]

Although there has been more federal aid available for more intensive housing-code enforcement, the problem remains to be solved. For even though there has been extensive investigation into the problem of housing, the tenants have suffered the burden. Im-proved housing conditions brought about by public action mean higher rent and a greater increase in the number of tenants moving. Accord-ing to Perry Ottenberg: "These very programs designed to help these areas can intensify the sense of alienation, apathy and underlying hostility in the population."[7] It seems reasonable to assume that re-housing programs need to convey much more sensitivity when dealing with America's social welfare.

Perhaps one of the earliest studies concerned specifically with the social effects of housing was the study conducted by Chapin. [8] This study was an attempt to measure the effects of good housing upon former slum families rehoused in the Summer Field Home of Missouri. The major hypothesis was that the rehousing of slum families in a public housing project results in the improvement of living conditions and the social life of these families. Scales were developed by Chapin to measure morale, general adjustment, social participation, and social status. Utilizing a quasi-experimental method, 108 project families were assigned to the "experimental group," and 131 families to the "control group." Using a matched-frequency distribution, the families were paired on the following characteristics: race, employment, occupational class, number of persons in the family, and income. The major hypotheses of the study were upheld, since the experimental group members (project families) showed significant gains over the control group on each of the dimensions considered previously.

Illustrative of the early focus on the relative importance of housing was the research by Reimer. [9] This research revealed that housing needs are dependent upon tradition, the family cycle, social status, personality traits, and patterns of dominance. Satisfactory home adjustment is achieved in two ways: (1) Through the tangible, objective part of physical shelter; and (2) by means of the more subjective part of the individual attitude and family behavior. [10]

In Louis Wirth's essay on housing, three significant aspects were considered relevant to sociological inquiry. [11] One aspect treats housing as a value and attempts to identify the specific content of the value it constitutes for different individuals and groups in society. Another consideration is to view the relationship between housing and the community, since the house does not stand by itself in an urban community. The third aspect is the relationship between housing and social policy. The focus here is on meeting the housing needs and expectations of people, since these needs and expectations are increasingly affected by factors over which the individual has little control (i.e., forced displacement).

In the early fifties, Bauer attempted to stimulate research emphasizing the need for studying habits, attitudes, and values of individuals as they are influenced by the housing environment:

> To gauge needs, we should know a great deal more than
> we do about people's behavior, welfare, and under differ-
> ent external conditions . . . research should distinguish
> between average behavior and attitudes under status quo
> conditions, and emerging trends in social values and
> activities, which may often require testing under new and

experimental conditions. . . . When people move, they
have reached a conscious decision strong enough to make
them act. Their reactions to past conditions and their
hopes and expectations for the future are relatively
crystallized. [12]

In a later study by Chapin, [13] three assumptions obtained: (1)
A "value system" in which adequate housing as a means contributes
to good mental health or hygiene as the end; (2) a cause-effect assumption in which the architects, builders, and planners possess the ability
to produce the effect desired by control or planned treatment of the
dwelling; and (3) the assumption that we can isolate the physical factors
of housing that condition emotional and mental responses. This last
assumption embraces the idea that physical factors can be separated
from three constellations of social factors—the "household group"
cluster of roles that exist in the dwelling. Chapin's conclusion was
that good housing promotes satisfactory individual adjustment. [14] The
study also emphasized the need for experimental designs and the construction of valid and reliable measuring devices for studying the effects
of housing on individual behavior.

In an attempt to utilize the experimental method recommended
by Chapin, Mogey conducted a study of the changes in the family life
of English workers moving from the slums to housing estates. A
random sample of 30 families was selected. Mogey's conclusions
were as follows:

The study strongly suggests that living on a municipal
housing estate alters many attitudes of the urban family.
In the first place—there is a tendency for the conjugal
type family to discover itself and for the obligations of
kinship to be relaxed. Secondly, relations between
neighbors undergo various subtle changes. Thirdly, the
family seems to acquire a new relationship to the city;
the location of friends in widely separated districts of the
city and the joining of societies show that the family members have ceased to show their loyalty to a kinship group
or neighborhood and to be on the way to becoming citizens
of a city. [15]

It is generally recognized that limited improvement in new
housing projects can be expected to produce a profound effect on the
physical and social stability of culturally deprived individuals. As
such, Robert Rice, through the Head Start Program, provided a
controlled condition for studying these effects on 208 black preschool
children from two housing projects in Kansas City. Accordingly, Rice
concluded that these children would represent the most sensitive

indicators of the effects of environmental influence, and inferred the
following: (1) A stimulating atmosphere can compensate for other
disadvantages produced in the slums. (2) The significance of this
atmosphere as a factor in human growth is inconclusive. (3) The
housing environment may provide a basic setting for further influencing
variables. [16]

Moreover, according to the President's Commission on Income
Maintenance Program, evidence exists both to support and to deny
the statement that housing should complement any income maintenance
program. Those who argue for housing suggest that it is one of the
primary contributors to the vicious cycle of poverty. They suggest
that overcrowding, typically associated with ghetto housing, is related
to stress and problems of self-perception. These inferences suggest
founded reasons for further study of the environmental effects of
housing. [17]

In an effort to relate housing characteristics to social disorganization, Loring used an ex post facto experimental design. [18] Low-
quality housing was defined by Loring in terms of lack of privacy,
overcrowding of interior space, land congestion, poor sanitary facilities, and poor maintenance and deterioration. His study suggests
that (1) physical characteristics of housing can be a factor in producing
problems related to social disorganization as the density ratio increases; (2) the density relevant to the systems observed in this
study is social density, definable in terms of social or cultural roles
simultaneously acting in a given space; and (3) overdensity present
in housing or neighborhood space may aggravate or accelerate, not
cause or motivate, any tendency to disorganization in a personality
or group. [19]

The most significant impact on this work was by a longitudinal
study of the housing environment and family life conducted from Johns
Hopkins University. [20] Researchers studied two groups of blacks.
One group was moved to new housing, while the other group remained
in slum housing. The major hypothesis considered was that the different housing quality of the two groups would be associated with
differences in behavior and attitude. Families in the control group,
which remained in the slums, were matched with families in the
test group according to amount of rent paid, size of dwelling unit,
and other factors. Measurements of overall quality of housing and
person-room density were used as criteria for estimating housing
quality. Various census data were also used to aid in determining
results of the study.

Examination of several behavioral factors and attitudes indicated
that the great majority of the reactions of test group members were

in the hypothesized direction. Results of questionnaires revealed-
that test families were found to be more satisfied with their apartments,
and that the amount of space was more satisfactory. This group's
members also interacted more with neighbors, felt themselves to be
more upwardly mobile, became more active in community affairs, and
were more well-adjusted as far as aggression and self-control were
concerned. [21] Studies cited below produced both similar and conflicting
results.

Accordingly, a Harvard University study attempted to exploit a
design for planning a compact city. A group of prominent regional
scientists under the direction of George J. Pillorge reasoned that the
quality of planning was of the utmost importance in designing such a
city. Moreover, these men envisioned the physical environment as a
catalyst for changing the basic design of the community. Their conclusions were as follows:

> From there we see society branching out qualitatively to
> increased appreciation for study, for self-development,
> for communicating with nature. . . . These are the
> directions that we are heading into and this permits
> smaller groups of people to live together at the highest
> level of personal and social development. [22]

Another study conducted earlier by Wilner and others has sought
to validate the same hypothesis and determine how better housing is
related to better adjustment. [23] Mogey's study of English families in
poor housing areas and housing projects suggests, as the others have,
that family members in the better housing area tend to become more
effective citizens. [24]

Conflicting research such as that conducted by Gans has produced different results. His research showed that moves to the
suburbs from the city do not create many behavioral changes. This
led him to assume that housing and the community do not significantly
affect people's lives and that social class, age, and other factors affect behavior patterns to a greater extent. [25]

Similarly, Mitchell's study was an attempt to ascertain the
effects, if any, that different dimensions of housing, especially density, have upon interacting family members. [26] The multistage sampling plan consisted of all individuals 18 years of age and over, drawn
from the urban area of Hong Kong. Furthermore, attitudinal scales
were developed and administered in order to ascertain (1) the dissatisfaction about the amount of space people have and (2) their feelings
toward their lack of privacy. Mitchell concluded that individuals can
tolerate very high densities within their own family dwelling unit, but

the emotional strain from such existence may create a street environment that is socially unhealthy for the community. [27]

Studies on the social effects of displacement have been numerous,
as have discussions on the good and bad consequences of voluntary and
involuntary movements. [28] Effects on the aged and on racial minorities
moved into integrated areas have been of primary interest. A study
by Goldstein and Zimmer indicated that a move is likely to create
serious problems of adjustment for older persons and disrupt their
way of life much more than the way of life of younger persons, who
are able to adjust more easily. [29] Research concerned with the
hypothesis that black tenants who live in integrated housing have more
positive self-concepts than those in segregated housing has yielded
only tentative results. [30]

Social disorganization and its relation to housing has been the
subject of several interesting studies. William C. Loring sought to
explain the fact that only particular families in a bad housing area
become disorganized. Results indicated that overcrowding, which
arises continually, may aggravate any tendency toward disorganization
a person or group may have. [31] Evidence supporting the belief that
juvenile delinquency, illness, and various forms of social disorganization are related to inadequate housing has also been produced.
Whether housing is a causal factor or merely an important link in a
chain of causal factors has not been resolved.

HOME OWNERSHIP

In studying the social effects of housing, it is necessary to include the role of home ownership. Much of the research concerned
with the ownership variable has been devoted to the discovery of the
housing ambitions of people and the ways in which these ambitions
are realized among different groups in society.

The American ideal indicates that home ownership is a desirable
goal, and although underlying motives may be diverse, Americans do
prefer to own their own homes. [32] Various studies have indicated ego
satisfaction, family security, psychic security, desire for high status,
security in old age, and amenities such as gardening as the goals of
ownership. Thus, social and psychological factors play an important
role in the decision to purchase a home, just as do economic reasons.

In view of the 1967 Detroit riot, one finds the need for a more
concentrated view of the neighborhood in the black ghetto. Evidence
supports the view that the life-style of a culture, measured by the
area of residence and condition of home, is a key social unit in

maintaining cohesive social interaction. [33] As such, it becomes possible to infer that the environmental effects of overcrowding, tension, and unemployment may become, if they are not already, a causal factor in the decision to purchase a home in such areas.

Research has also borne out the expectation that more homeowners are churchgoers, union members, and voters; and, that families with different interests and activities, incomes and abilities, buy houses. Our understanding of the reasons for these actions, however, is not well developed. [34]

One of the early studies concerned with home ownership was conducted by Caplow. [35] This study was part of a larger study of residential mobility, and the results were based on the housing histories of a stratified sample of 574 Minneapolis families. An overwhelming portion (91.1 percent) were found to favor home ownership for themselves and home ownership in general. Also, homeowners expressed themselves consistently more satisfied with their own housing arrangements than did tenants. Moreover, those who had been owners as early as 1940 were somewhat more satisfied than those who shifted from tenancy to ownership during wartime or in the postwar period. In Caplow's words:

> The difference between tenants and owners are entirely consistent, and for the most part, statistically significant. On each of the five items, tenants evinced conspicuously more dissatisfaction than owners. The incomplete evidence which follows suggests that this difference is not primarily a function of socioeconomic differences between the two groups, but also reflects the pattern of attitudes favoring ownership, and the unavailability of rental units of good quality under current conditions. . . . these differences must be derived from the cluster of values associated with ownership. [36]

The cluster of values surrounding home ownership is the result of the aspirations of most Americans to own their own home. This aspiration was succinctly epitomized in President Hoover's solemn verdict: ". . . to possess one's own home is the hope and ambition of almost every individual in our country—that our people should live in their own homes is a sentiment deep in the heart of our race and American life. "[37]

Irving Rosow indicates that estimates of the extent of this hope vary between 65 percent and 89 percent, depending upon the sample tested and the structure of the investigation. [38] In his study, the previous research on ownership motives was summarized as follows:

(1) sentiments of possessing property, individualism, independence; (2) financial goals of investment, long-range
economy, old-age security; (3) family aims of status,
stability, having a desired kind of house, a desired
children's environment. [39]

In Dean's study of home ownership, it is suggested that two
basic values enter the home ownership pattern. These values are
imbedded in the middle-class Protestant ethic and classical econom-
ics. [40] Dean elaborates on these values in the following statement:

For many families of modest income, home ownership
today represents a step up into middle-class respectabil-
ity. But middle-class aspirations in our society are often
supported by the Protestant ethic: higher status and standard of living are individual responsibilities; they are the
result of hard work, thrift, ingenuity, and self-denial;
property is viewed as the fruit of individual effort, and
its accumulation is supported to reflect moral integrity
and reliable work habits. [41]

Most American families prefer to own their homes. We know
that families with different interests and activities, with different
incomes and abilities, do purchase, and, at different stages of development, attempt to purchase, homes under varying market conditions.
According to Dean, however, we know next to nothing about how these
various elements are perceived by different types of home purchasers
and how they relate to the satisfaction of housing needs.

In a more recent study, Coons and Glaze point out that the
purpose of home ownership is the direct satisfaction of wants and
that many of these wants are of a noneconomic nature. [42] In analyzing
the reasons for home ownership, two reasons appear most frequently:
(1) Security of residence provided by home ownership; and (2) the
desire to accumulate a savings, to build up equity.[43]

Abrams, focusing attention on the meaning of home ownership
for the lower socioeconomic strata, states: "To the poorer family,
home ownership is a prime hope, representing not only shelter but
life-long security. "[44]

In another study, Shinn sought to analyze 20 white college
students between the ages of 18 and 27 with no children. [45] The advantage of this sample was the ability to account for all variables
relevant to the utility of housing. According to a multiple nonlinear
regression-type model, Shinn showed that general desirability was

related to type, space, price, and quality of a home. Further
inferences show the relevance of socioeconomic factors are related
to home ownership.

Another study, done by Lander, related socioeconomic and
anomic variables to delinquency. In the anomic cluster of variables,
Lander classified the lack of home ownership as being a measure of
family instability. Also, Lander found that those areas with low per-
centages of home ownership had high delinquency rates. [46]

In Morris and Mogey's project, the authors interviewed rehoused
wartime squatters and further analyzed the effects of satisfying levels
of social and community relations to which they were exposed. [47]
Three waves of interviews were administered to a relocated experimental group and a control group not yet moved. Moreover, these
schedules focused on attitudes and perceptions of housing, wider
community relations, and the surrounding neighborhood situations.
Accordingly, the study showed that the best-adjusted residents were
those who were satisfied with rent and housing. Adjustment was also
related to working in the city, complimentary wage scale, and membership in a club. Finally, the authors concluded that the neighborhood unit theory was inadequate, noting that intimacy may be recipro-
cally related to friction as well as to friendship.

Finally, a study of black families facing relocation was conducted
by Lewis Watts and others in a section of Boston that was involved in
a massive program of urban renewal. The researchers began the
study with the hypothesis that all of the families involved would move
from the area if given the chance. Findings indicated that younger
families who did not own their own homes planned to move, while
older home owners wanted to remain in their homes. This indication
of the desire for home ownership has been discovered in other studies
also. One interesting fact about this study is that the researchers
found, through later interviews, that very few of the families had
actually moved. This finding was attributed to economic reasons and
fear of prejudice. [48] Other studies of relocation have emphasized
the problems of finding satisfactory replacements for housing when
renewal is planned.

Cagle and Deutscher have concluded that urban renewal programs
have failed to provide adequate housing that meets the needs and de-
sires of relocated families. Moreover, these families expressed dissatisfaction with their neighbors and appeared less likely to move
elsewhere merely for family contact. They point out that "it appears
that when the situation is salient, people will tend to follow up on
their intentions. "[49]

Seemingly, the apathy of the community members often leads
to little constructive assistance to those to be moved and abets the
likelihood of choices of substandard housing. Often, shortages of
decent housing and prejudice contribute to the problem. Watts's
study emphasizes the general indifference of the public toward helping
these people. 50

Thus, it appears that social and psychological implications of
home ownership seem to be many and are perhaps indicative of certain
aspects of all social problems. An understanding of these implications
would certainly facilitate more satisfactory adjustment among the relocated and various social classes and racial groups in the United
States.

SUMMARY

The problems associated with inadequate housing have been
studied by researchers with varied results. Whether inadequate
housing causes delinquency, disorganization, and so forth, or is
merely a link in a chain of factors, has not been determined. Indications do point to the influence that overcrowding and inadequate living
facilities have on the attitudes and feelings of people who live in such
circumstances. Resulting feelings of alienation and social isolation
have been emphasized and studied.

Attention in this study is focused on individuals who have experienced a change in housing tenure and an improved quality of housing in order to determine what effects these changes would have on
the people involved. A number of studies, such as Chapin's and
Mogey's, have focused on this same problem. A study conducted by
Johns Hopkins University had the most significant impact on the
present study. In the study, families in a control group remained
living in the slums and were matched with families moved to new
housing. Indications were that more of the test families were satisfied and well-adjusted.

The desire for home ownership, which is prevalent in our society, has often been related to the ways this goal is realized and to
housing aspirations. Several studies have shown tha the overwhelming proportion of people prefer to own their own homes. This goal
of home ownership seems to be especially important to poorer families.
It is felt that a greater understanding of the implications of home ownership would aid the social adjustment of relocated groups.

NOTES

1. M. S. Gorovosov, "The Physiological Basis of Health Standards for Dwellings, " Public Health Papers, No. 33 (1968), pp. 87-89.

2. Kent Rice, "Survival in Adversity: A Study of Family Health and Poverty" (Little Rock: Arkansas Health Planning Program, 1968), pp. 9-10.

3. Walter Bar, "Planning and the Home Environment: London Regional Conference Report, " Housing, 7, 1 (May, 1971).

4. Robert K. Merton, "The Social Psychology of Housing, " in Current Trends in Social Psychology, ed. by Wayne Dennis, (Pittsburgh: University of Pittsburgh Press, 1951), p. 165.

5. Daniel M. Wilner et al., The Housing Environment and Family Life (Baltimore: The Johns Hopkins Press, 1962) pp. 3-18.

6. Catherine Bauer, "Some Questions in Housing and Community Planning, " Journal of Social Issues, VII, 1 (1951), pp. 1-34.

7. Perry Ottenberg, M. D., "Dehumanization in Social Planning and Community Psychiatry", American Journal of Psychotherapy, 22 (1968), p. 589.

8. F. S. Chapin, "An Experiment on the Social Effects of Good Housing, " American Sociological Review, V (December, 1940), pp. 868-79.

9. Svend Reimer, "Sociological Theory of Home Adjustment, " American Sociological Research, VIII (June, 1943), pp. 272-78.

10. Ibid.

11. Louis Wirth, "Housing As a Field of Sociological Research, " American Sociological Review, XII (April, 1947), pp. 137-43.

12. Bauer, op. cit., p. 7.

13. F. S. Chapin, "Some Housing Factors Related to Mental Hygiene," American Journal of Public Health, XLI (1951), pp. 839-45.

14. Ibid., p. 842.

15. J. M. Mogey, "Changes in Family Life Experienced by English Workers Moving from Slums to Housing Estates, " Marriage and Family Living, XVII (1955), p. 128.

16. Robert R. Rice, "The Effects of Project Head Start and Differential Housing Environments Upon Child Development, " The Family Coordinator: Journal of Education, Counseling and Services, 18, 1 (January, 1969), pp. 32-38.

17. The President's Commission on Income Maintenance Programs, "Housing, " Background Papers (Minneapolis, Minnesota: National Council on Family Relations, 1970), pp. 94-96.

18. William C. Loring, Jr., "Housing Characteristics and Social Disorganization, " Social Problems, III (January, 1956), pp. 160-68.

19. Ibid.

20. Wilner, op. cit., pp. 3-18.

21. Ibid.

22. Edward G. Echwerria, Summary of a Statement of the Howard University Study, June 1968, in Maryland National Capital Park and Planning Commission, "The Quality of Urban Life," (Washington, D.C., 1970) pp. 459-556.

23. D. M. Wilner, R. P. Walkely, and M. Tayback, "How Does the Quality of Housing Affect Health and Family Adjustment?" American Journal of Public Health, XLVI (1956), pp. 736-44.

24. Mogey, op. cit., pp. 123-32.

25. Herbert J. Gans, "Effects of the Move from City to Suburb, " in Leonard I. Duhl, ed., The Urban Condition (New York: Basic Books, 1963), pp. 184-98.

26. Robert Edward Mitchell, "Some Social Implications of High Density Housing, " American Sociological Review, 36 (February, 1971) 1, pp. 18-29.

27. Ibid.

28. It has been estimated that following the Housing Act of 1949, only 66,000 families were displaced by governmental action

during the first ten years. However, the pace of urban renewal is now quickening, and so is the highway express system. As a result, the future national rate of involuntary displacement is estimated at more than 150,000 families per year. See U.S. Senate, Subcommittee of the Committee on Banking and Currency, Study of Mortgage Credit, 86th Cong., 1st sess., p. 37.

29. Sidney Goldstein and Basil Zimmer, Residential Displacements and Resettlement of the Aged: A Study of Problems of Rehousing Aged Residents Displaced by Freeway Construction in Downtown Providence, (Providence: Rhode Island Division on Aging Population, 1960).

30. Ernest Works, "Residence in Integrated and Segregated Housing and Improvement in Self-Concepts of Negroes," Sociology and Social Research, XLVI (April, 1962), pp. 224-30.

31. Loring, op. cit., pp. 160-68.

32. Lawrence T. Cagle and Irwin Deutscher, Housing Aspirations of Low-Income Fatherless Families (Mimeographed paper, Syracuse University Youth Development Center, n.d.), p. 22.

33. Donald I. Warren, "Neighborhood Structure and Riot Behavior in Detroit: Some Exploratory Findings," Social Problems, 16, 4 (Spring, 1969), pp. 464-84.

34. John P. Dean, "The Ghosts of Home Ownership," Journal of Social Issues, VII, 1 (1951), pp. 59-68.

35. Theodore Caplow, "Home Ownership and Location Preferences in a Minneapolis Sample," American Sociological Review, XIII (December, 1948), pp. 725-30.

36. Ibid., p. 728.

37. Opening Address by Herbert Hoover at the President's Conference on Home Building and Home Ownership, Washington, D.C., December 2, 1931 (as reported in the U.S. Daily, December 4, 1931 Vol. 11).

38. Irving Rosow, "Home Ownership Motives," American Sociological Review, XIII, 6 (December, 1948), pp. 751-56.

39. Ibid., p. 752.

40. Dean, op. cit., pp. 59-68.

41. Ibid., p. 59.

42.   Alvin E. Coons and Bert T. Glaze, Housing Market Analysis and the Growth of Nonfarm Home Ownership (Bureau of Business Research Monograph No. 115, Ohio State University, 1968), p. 7.

43.   Charles Abrams, Man's Struggle for Shelter in an Urbanizing World (Cambridge: The M.I.T. Press, 1964), p. 221.

44.   Ibid., p. 130.

45.   Allen M. Shinn, Jr., "Measuring the Utility of Housing; Demonstrating a Methodological Approach," Social Science Quarterly, 52, 1 (June 1971), pp. 88-102.

46.   Bernard Lander, Toward an Understanding of Juvenile Delinquency (New York: Columbia University Press, 1954).

47.   Raymond N. Morris and John M. Mogey, The Sociology of Housing: Studies at Baringfield, " (New York: The Humanities Press, 1965).

48.   Lewis Watts et al., The Middle-Income Negro Family Faces Urban Renewal (Research Center of the Florence Hellar Graduate School for Advanced Studies in Social Welfare, Brandeis University, 1964).

49.   Lawrence T. Cagle and Jewin Deutscher. "Housing Aspirations and Housing Achievements: The Relocation of Poor Families, " Social Problems, 18, 2 (Fall, 1970), pp. 243-56.

50.   Harry Reynolds, "What Do We Know About Our Experiences With Relocation?" Journal of Intergroup Relations, II, 4, (Autumn, 1961), pp. 342-54.

The main concern of this chapter is to present a conceptual scheme for evaluating the effects of change in tenure and quality of housing on the social adjustment of dislocated slum dwellers. The first section focuses on a theoretical discussion of social adjustment. The second section is concerned with developing testable propositions to be analyzed in Chapter 5.

SOCIAL ADJUSTMENT

Various studies in the past have been concerned with social and psychological adjustment. Found in these studies is the concept that social adjustment is measurable by the degree of social pathology among samples of individuals. The most frequently used concepts that appear to be indicants of social pathology are alienation and anomie. We therefore focus on alienation and anomie theory for a frame of reference to investigate social adjustment.

Alienation and Anomie Theory

Alienation and anomie are concepts that appear frequently to describe the psychological and social adjustment characterictic of modern industrialized societies. Beginning with Marx, whose theoretical perspective on alienation was political, the history of the definitive usages of the terms alienation and anomie have been varied.

Most of the theoretical formulations on alienation have been based on the works of Marx and Durkheim, who believed that alienation is caused by social and cultural structures and that an individual is formed largely by the norms and mores of his society. Marx reasoned that conflict in any society is caused by conflict between two classes—the bourgeoisie and the proletariat.[1] This, he felt, produces alienation of the worker, especially if his work is of a menial nature. Durkheim believed that alienation can be defined as a lack of norms or a feeling that norms of society have nothing to do with one's life.[2]

In summarizing the research and theoretical speculation on alienation, Besag states:

> Theories and research in the field of alienation fall roughly into three categories: (1) value-oriented formulations which attempt to change the social structure or cultural structure; (2) non-value-oriented formulations which attempt to determine the parameters of alienation without regard to the effect of their work upon the social or cultural structure; and (3) compilatory and encyclopedic formulations which attempt to reorganize the theories of other men.[3]

According to John Merton, alienation for Marx and anomie for Durkheim were metaphors for a radical attack on the dominant institutions and values of industrialized societies. Durkheim believed, for example, that the social state of normlessness, or anomie, has become institutionalized in the economic way of life. For Marx, the economic doctrine of self-interest is one indication of alienation, self-estrangement, and powerlessness in a capitalist society; and for Durkheim, the same thing indicates anomie, a problem of inadequate, rather than illegitimate, social control.[4] After study, it becomes apparent that anomie as Durkheim conceived it in the subjective sense has three characteristics: (1) a painful uneasiness or anxiety; (2) a feeling of separation from the group or of isolation from the group standards; and (3) a feeling of pointlessness or that no clearly defined goals exist.[5]

Because people are goal-directed, the inability to achieve desired goals, or an uncertainty of suitable methods to use in achieving them if they have been defined, often causes problems of orientation for individuals in a specified social system. For example, middle-class anomie is likely to result primarily from strain associated with disparity between aspirations and achievement. Lower-class anomie, on the other hand, is more likely to represent strain associated with both limits on opportunities for integration into community life and limits on occupational attainment.[6] Mizruchi found that when occupational achievement seems to be blocked, the middle-class members become more demoralized than the lower classes. This led him to conclude that there are various types of anomie distributed among

the classes.[7] Among Ephraim H. Mizruchi's many works on anomie
is a study conducted in a small city. In this particular study, more
than 600 household heads were interviewed using the Hollingshed
ISP, a modified Chapin scale, and the Srole scale, along with other
measures. Findings revealed a significant relationship of anomia to
class identification and social participation. The lower-class members
of the sample tended to be more anomic because of lack of opportunity
to achieve goals and different access to supportive subsystems.[8]

Meier and Bell, in another study, proposed the hypothesis that
limitations in American social structure limit access to means of
goal achievement. Their findings indicated that opportunity is inversely related to degree of anomie.[9]

Hypotheses have been supported by empirical data that there
are negative correlations between alienation and social status and
between alienation and advancing age.[10] Reasons given for these
correlations vary. Members of the lower class may misunderstand
situations; people of higher status attempt to limit their access to
higher status; obstacles of all sorts may be placed in their path.[11]
In any industrialized society, a large proportion of the population
must engage in some type of repetitive work. From feels that as
meaningless work increases, as it has in the United States, so does
estrangement from work and alienation.[12]

According to Seeman, alienation may be conceived as being a
form of powerlessness, or the belief that one's own behavior cannot
determine the outcome he seeks; meaninglessness, or low expectancy
about prediction of future outcomes; normlessness, or high expectancy
that socially unapproved behaviors are required to achieve goals;
isolation, or the belief that goals highly regarded in society are of
low reward value; and self-estrangement, or dependence on given
behavior upon anticipation of future rewards.[13]

The results of the effects of alienation and anomie can be seen
especially in slum or lower-income areas. The people in such areas
tend to be isolated from things that make for the integration of people
in dynamic, mutually reinforcing social and economic systems. They
may be socially or ideologically alienated or both.[14]

Merton has relied on both Marx and Durkheim. He defines
alienation as the conflict of the individual with societal goals and
places blame on society for turning an individual against himself.[15]
His definition of anomie is "a breakdown in the cultural structure,
occurring particularly where there is an acute disjunction between
cultural norms and goals and the socially structured capacities of
members of the group to act in accord with them."[16] As one of his

major achievements, Merton categorized types of adaptations to
anomic situations. The five modes of adaptation he gives are con-
formity, innovation, ritualism, retreatism, and rebellion. [17] Slum
dwellers and persons who live in poor-quality housing react to their
surroundings in these ways.

The hypothesis that isolated and alienated individuals are more
prone to extremism has been supported in studies of Negro males
living in integrated and segregated areas. Those in the segregated
areas view violence as more necessary than do those tied more firmly
to the society. The situation of the black in American society is one
extremely conducive to feelings of alienation. Members of the Negro
race suffer the consequences of discrimination, and their self-esteem
suffers. They may suppress their frustration or become resentful,
submissive, or ingratiating. [18]

In another study of Americans of European descent, or Anglos,
Spanish-speaking people, and Utes, conducted in the Southwest, researchers found that Anglos exhibited less anomie than did the minority groups. The availability of illegitimate means was also positively
related to deviant behavior. [19]

In our success-oriented society, the inability to achieve the
desired success, for whatever reasons, leads to anomie. In one
study, home ownership was selected as one of the most important
symbols. [20] This attribution of success to home owners leads to
the question of what effects change in tenure has on the degree of
alienation in individuals.

A STATEMENT OF THE CONCEPTUAL SCHEME

The most immediate matter of concern in sociology is to find
a way to link social and cultural variables to sociological theory.
This means that behavioral responses must be treated systematically
within a conceptual model rather than in ad hoc descriptive fashion.
It is evident that this requires theory to be grounded in empirical
reality. This is the position taken in this research.

In the review of research and theoretical arguments concerned
with variables related to or producing alienation in society, it was
found that these factors are most frequently of a social, economic,
and social-psychological nature. Thus, we can assume that when an
individual feels that the forces in society are operating to improve
his opportunities, his alienation is reduced, and, consequently, he
is more firmly integrated into the social system.

In urban America, the slum areas of the city represent the end of the line for a large portion of the population. The crucial element here is that the inhabitants of slum areas feel this way about themselves. The reasons for this feeling of despair can be summed up by looking at the identifiable features of the slum: (1) absolute or relative poverty; (2) deteriorated housing; (3) overcrowding, (4) a high concentration of lower-class blacks; (5) high crime rates; (6) health problems; (7) broken families; (8) relocation problems; and (9) inadequate community services. Thus, in a social and physical environment typified by these features, it not unlikely that the inhabitants are not socially adjusted. Social adjustment is viewed in terms of the degree of alienation expressed by the individual.

Alienation, then, or its reduction, is the focus of this inquiry. Alienation is assumed to be a multidimensional attitudinal set that is measurable by the degrees of anomie, social isolation, and sense of powerlessness. It is further assumed that three factors, not entirely independent, can produce a reduction in alienation toward society. The most important factor is home ownership. On-the-site observation by this researcher resulted in the conclusion that, in every case, the quality of the houses of homeowners was superior to the quality of renters' houses. The other two factors, neighborhood satisfaction and social participation, are logically related to the degree of alienation.

The next section is concerned with the major concepts used in this study.

MAJOR CONCEPTS

Tenure and Housing Quality

Since this research is concerned with the relationship between quality of the housing environment and social adjustment, tenure is the most important variable considered in the analysis. In this research, tenure was operationalized by asking the respondents if they rented or if they were purchasing a house. Those that indicated they were renters and owners were so classified. Data in Chapter 5 support the proposition that the quality of the housing environment of homeowners is substantially better than that of the renters.

Social Participation

The Chapin social participation scale was used in this research. A brief description of this scale indicates that the following criteria

were used as indicants of the intensity of involvement of individuals
in the community. These indicants are type of voluntary organization,
attendance schedule, contribution, and offices held. The traditional
scoring procedure suggested by Chapin was used.

Neighborhood Satisfaction

In an attempt to develop a reliable indicator of neighborhood
satisfaction, a Guttman-type scale[21] composed of five items served
to measure the respondent's degree of satisfaction with his local
community.

Respondents were asked to indicate how they felt about certain
dimensions of their neighborhood sphere. The questions used were

1. Are you anxious to stay here (move out), or doesn't it matter
   much to you?

2. Are you satisfied with this location as related to nearness to
   friends and relatives?

3. How do you feel about the recreational facilities such as parks,
   playgrounds, and swimming pools?

4. How do you feel about police protection and services?

5. How do you feel about the opportunities to find good housing?

Social Adjustment

Several attempts have been made to define social adjustment.
These efforts depend primarily on the orientation of the researcher,
for example, psychological, social-psychological, sociological. In
this research, social adjustment is defined in terms of anomie,
powerlessness, and social isolation. Several other attitudinal items
are also included in the analysis.

Anomie

The five-item anomie scale developed by Leo Srole was used
to measure anomie as perceived by the respondents in this study.
The items are as follows:

1. I worry about the future facing today's children.

2. We are just so many cogs in the machinery of life.

3. Most people don't really care what happens to the next fellow.

4. Sometimes I feel all alone in the world.

5. No one really understands me.

Social Isolation

Social isolation is the feeling of being separated or isolated from the group. It also entails the idea of being rejected by one's peers. The five items below were used by Dean in his attempt to measure social isolation.

1. Most people today seldom feel lonely.

2. Real friends are as easy as ever to find.

3. One can always find friends if he shows himself friendly.

4. The world in which we live is basically a friendly place.

5. I think single life is better than married life.

Powerlessness

Powerlessness has been defined by Marx and others as a feeling of helplessness and a lack of control over work that appears to be characteristic of most jobholders in industrial societies. In an effort to measure this dimension of alienation, a five-item scale was constructed. This scale was also used by Dean. The items are as follows:

1. There is little chance to get a promotion on the job unless a man gets a break.

2. There is little or nothing I can do towards preventing a major "shooting war."

3. Sometimes I have the feeling other people are using me.

4. The future looks very dismal.

5. To make money, there are no right and wrong ways any more, only easy ways and hard ways.

THEORETICAL PROPOSITIONS

The major proposition in this research is that tenure and quality of the housing environment are related to social adjustment. The following major hypotheses are tested:

1. Tenure is related to

    (a) housing quality and

    (b) social adjustment.

2. Social participation is positively related to social adjustment.

3. Neighborhood satisfaction is positively related social adjustment.

Subhypotheses tested in this research are

1. Tenure explains a significant proportion of the variation in

    (a) anomie,

    (b) social isolation, and

    (c) powerlessness.

2. Neighborhood satisfaction explains a significant proportion of the variation in

    (a) social adjustment,

    (b) anomie,

    (c) social isolation, and

    (d) powerlessness.

3. Social participation explains a significant proportion of the variation in

    (a) social adjustment,

    (b) anomie,

    (c) social isolation, and

    (d) powerlessness.

SUMMARY

This chapter is concerned with stating explicitly the conceptual and theoretical perspectives derived from the review of relevant literature. It also serves to provide theoretical direction for the research. In addition to a discussion of the methodological procedures employed, the analytical strategy for the empirical part of the dissertation is expressly set forth in Chapter 4.

NOTES

1.   Karl Marx, Selected Writings in Sociological and Social Philosophy, trans. T. B. Bottomore (New York: McGraw-Hill, 1964), p. 128.

2.   Emile Durkheim, Suicide, trans. John A. Spaulding and George Simpson (New York: The Free Press, 1951), p. 45.

3.   Frank P. Besag, Alienation and Education, An Empirical Approach (Buffalo, New York: Hertillon Press, 1966), p. 2.

4.   John Horton, "The Dehumanization of Anomie and Alienation: A Problem in the Ideology of Sociology," British Journal of Sociology, XV (1964), pp. 284-308.

5.   Emile Durkheim, op. cit., p. 45.

6.   Ephraim H. Mizruchi, Success and Opportunity: A Study of Anomie (New York: Free Press of Glencoe, 1964), p. 117.

7.   Ibid., p. 127.

8.   Ephraim H. Mizruchi, "Social Structure and Anomie in a Small City," American Sociological Review, XXV (October, 1960), 45-54.

9.   Dorothy Meier and Wendell Bell, "Anomie and Differential Access to the Achievement of Life Goals," American Sociological Review XXIV (April, 1959), 189-202.

10.   Dwight Dean, "Alienation: Its Meaning and Measurement," American Sociological Review, XXVI (October, 1961), 753-758.

11.   Mizruchi, Success and Opportunity, p. 116.

12. Eric Fromm, The Sane Society (New York: Holt, Rinehart and Winston, 1955).

13. Melvin Seeman, "On the Meaning of Alienation," American Sociological Review, XXII (December, 1957), 783-91.

14. Ritchie Lowry, "The Functions of Alienation in Leadership," Sociology and Social Research, XLVI (July, 1962), 426-35.

15. Robert K. Merton, Social Theory and Social Structure (rev. ed., Glencoe, Ill. The Free Press, 1957), p. 163.

16. Ibid., p. 162.

17. Ibid., pp. 141-59.

18. Robin Williams, American Society (rev. ed., New York: Alfred A. Knopf, 1960), p. 543.

19. Robert Hanson and Theodore D. Graves, "Objective Access, Anomie, and Deviance in a Tri-Ethnic Community" (Paper presented at the Meeting of the American Sociological Association, Los Angeles, August, 1963).

20. Mizruchi, Success and Opportunity, p. 72.

21. Louis Guttman, Measurement and Prediction, of "Studies in Social Psychology in World War II," IV (Princeton: Princeton University Press, 1950), Chapters 3 and 4.

4

INTRODUCTION

The purpose of this chapter is to discuss the factors that gave impetus to the study, and to give a description of the general housing conditions existing in the metropolitan area, with a specific focus on housing conditions in predominantly black areas. Techniques of data collection are described. In addition, a discussion of the procedures used to identify the sample population is given. Several attitudinal scales are presented along with the criteria of scalability. Finally, the analytical strategy is elaborated.

This work is a specific aspect of a much larger project concerning the study of community problems and the role of biracial committee in a southern metropolitan city. The investigators of the larger survey proposed to work closely with community leaders in developing and testing a model that would be enlightening to other communities. This project, sponsored by a grant from the Rockefeller Foundation, proposed the following types of studies:

1. A critical and detailed analysis of the current situation of the black population as reflected by such criteria as income, employment, housing, family disorganization, physical health, mental health, delinquency, and education.

2. A parallel analysis of the resources of the community such as clinics, counselors, school facilities, police services, and public or private welfare agencies, available to meet the needs of the black population.

3. Fact-finding in other areas of significance for race relations as requested by interested local citizens' groups.

4. A study of the differential effect of the desegregation crises on the functioning of the biracial committee and on race relations in the community.

5. A study of the structure of black leadership, its relationship to white leadership, and the extent and nature of the participation of black leaders in the formulation of policies and practices affecting their group.

6. Sample surveys of community attitudes toward services and facilities.

7. Feedback of research results into the community through either biracial or racially homogeneous leadership groups and simultaneous analysis of interaction within and between these groups. [1]

This work focuses on one aspect of Study 1, that is, a detailed analysis of the current housing situation; of Study 3, fact-finding resulting from the expressed interests of a subcommittee of the biracial committee on housing and relocation; and of Study 6, a sample survey of attitudes toward housing, home ownership, and other aspects of community life.

THE FIELD WORK SITE

Since the data obtained for this study were gathered at the request of the Committee on Housing, a subcommittee of the metropolitan Area Chamber of Commerce, it seems appropriate to describe the overall housing condition of this southern metropolitan area. Table 1 provides a summary of the housing conditions as they existed in 1950 and 1960.

It is apparent that, although the population in the central city has decreased slightly, the number of dwelling units increased by 15 percent. However, a close inspection of the data reveals that the number of sound units decreased by 3.3 percent. More significant is the change in the number of deteriorating and dilapidated houses. In 1950, 27.8 percent of the houses were classified in poor condition, while in 1960, the proportion increased to 30.3 percent. Of particular relevance to this study is the 16.4 percent increase in dwellings occupied by black Americans.

When attention is focused on the areas of the city that were predominantly black in 1950, we find that 53.5 percent of the housing was deteriorated or dilapidated. Also in 1950, 52 percent of the houses were occupied by black families. However, in 1960, in

TABLE 1

Summary of Characteristics of Housing Units
in Jacksonville, 1950 and 1960

Characteristic	1950		1960		Percent Change
	Number	Percent	Number	Percent	
Total Population	204,517	100.0	201,030	100.0	-1.7
Total Housing Units	58,718	100.0	67,522	100.0	15.0
Sound Units	42,395	72.2	47,115	69.8	-3.3
Deteriorating	8,007	13.6	14,696	21.8	60.3
Dilapidated	8,316	14.2	5,711	8.5	-40.1
Owner-occupied	28,115	46.5	30,995	49.7	6.9
Renter-occupied	29,792	49.3	31,406	50.3	2.0
Nonwhite-occupied	17,484	29.8	21,679	34.7	16.4

Source: U.S. Bureau of the Census, U.S. Census of Housing: 1960, vol. III, City Blocks, Series HC(3), No. 109 (Washington, D.C.: U.S. Government Printing Office, 1961).

approximately the same geographic area, 92 percent of the dwelling
units were occupied by black residents, illustrating, quite conclusively
the ecological process of invasion. Correspondingly, an equally high
proportion of the houses were classified as deteriorating or dilapidated

The information contained in Table 2 describes the housing
conditions of the area cleared by governmental action in order to
construct an expressway. In this ward, 74.1 percent of the houses
were classified as being in poor condition in 1950. There is no reason
to assume that the conditions improved prior to action taken by the
local officials of the municipality in 1958. Of extreme importance
to this study is the fact that ward 5 was 87.1 percent black, and, more
importantly, 91.6 percent of the dwellings were rented. These data
provide the basis for several assumptions considered in a subsequent
section of this research.

THE INTERVIEW SAMPLE

The primary purpose of the study was to establish whether the
individuals and/or families displaced when the expressway was being
built had found adequate housing. It should be noted that one of the
major grievances of black representatives on the biracial committee
was a concern for the 1700 families displaced by the expressway
authority.

The research project was directed by members of the Department
of Sociology and the staff of the Institute for Social Research, Florida
State University. This author served as field director. A simple
random sample was selected of individuals 21 years of age or older
who were displaced by the construction of the expressway. From the
files of the local housing authority, 1700 familes were identified.
The families were numbered and a 33 percent sample was drawn.
This resulted in a final sample of 549 household heads and/or their
spouses. All of the families had lived at one time in the area through
which the expressway passed and were now living in housing they had
acquired since the move. The interviewers went into the field during
the summer of 1962. Each interviewer underwent a two-week training
session conducted by the staff of the Institute for Social Research.
The interviewing was completed by September of 1962. Since the
sample consisted of black household heads, black interviewers were
used.

DESCRIPTION AND EVALUATION
OF MEASUREMENT

The design of this study required the measurement of several
independent and dependent variables. These measures are described
and evaluated in this section.

TABLE 2

Summary of Characteristics of Housing Units
for the Area Cleared by Expressway Authority,
(Ward 5), 1950

Characteristic	Number	Percent
Total Housing Units	3,968	100.0
Sound Units	1,024	25.9
Deteriorating	1,885	47.6
Dilapidated	1,049	26.5
Owner-occupied	344	8.7
Renter-occupied	3,626	91.6
Nonwhite-occupied	3,448	87.1

Source: Jacksonville, Florida U.S. Department of Commerce, Bureau of the Census, U.S. Census of Housing: 1960 (Washington, D.C.: Jacksonville, Florida U.S. Department of Commerce).

Independent Variables

The variables in this research that are considered to be causal factors in explaining social adjustment are tenure and quality of the housing environment, social participation, and neighborhood satisfaction.

Tenure

Tenure was determined by asking the respondents if they were renting or buying their present dwelling. They were also asked if they were renting or buying their previous dwelling. Only respondents who rented previously and were presently renting, and respondents previously renting and presently buying, were used in the analysis. Thus, the classifications of renter and owner were developed and used in the analysis.

Quality of Housing Environment

Quality of housing environment was measured in terms of the meaningful and tangible elements of the physical environment. Respondents were asked to indicate their satisfaction, dissatisfaction, or indifference to the following aspects of the physical environment:

amount of privacy, amount of closet space, heating and cooling equipment, street noise, air and sunlight, open space around the house, amount of room, and their feelings toward their new residence. For analytical purposes, the respondents indicating indifference were eliminated from the analysis.

Social Participation

The Chapin social participation scale was used in this research. This scale involves types of voluntary organizations, frequency of attendance, financial contributions, and offices held. That is, a score of 1 was given to each respondent for each organization of which he was a member, a score of 2 for regular attendance at meetings, a score of 3 for contributions, and a score of 4 for positions of officer or committee member. Therefore, the maximum score for each organization was 10. In the sample, the scores ranged from 0 to 10.

A recognized deficiency of this measure is that religion is considered in the analysis as an indicator of the intensity of community involvement. Several critics of Chapin's scale have indicated that this particular organizational involvement is not a valid indicator of social participation. To some extent, this criticism is justified. However, the church has traditionally been the focal point for all the organization, in the black community. Not only are religious services maintained in the black church, but also many other types of political, social, and economic activities are carried out within this institution.

For analytical purposes, the respondents were classified as participants and nonparticipants. This dichotomy removes some of the ambiguousness associated with the use of Chapin's social participation scale. Also, the statistical model employed in the analysis requires dichotomous variables.

Neighborhood Satisfaction

In an attempt to operationalize the neighborhood satisfaction, seven items that are logical indicants of the degree of relative contentment with one's neighborhood were extracted from the interview schedule. These items were presented in the theoretical discussion of the independent variables in Chapter 3.

In constructing an index of social phenomena, it is frequently necessary to combine several items to measure a construct. The combining items generally result in a type of scale. Thus, by scaling sociological constructs, researchers can define concepts mathematically as well as verbally and measure concepts that otherwise could not be measured directly.[2]

The use of scaling techniques permits the researcher to make distinctions of degree rather than quality. In almost all instances, it is more desirable to assert that one individual is more anomic than another individual, rather than being limited to the statement that they differ on anomie. [3]

In view of the need to combine qualitative attributes into a quantative variable, the Guttman technique was used. This technique seeks to find "pure" scales along a single continuum, so that a respondent who answers any one question favorably will answer favorably all items to which a favorable reply is more commonly given. [4] The important aspect about this pattern is that, if it holds, knowing an individual's score makes it possible to determine exactly which items were endorsed.

In practice, perfect cumulative or unidimensional scales are rarely if ever found in social research, although approximations can often be developed. Scalogram analysis uses several criteria for deciding if a series of items may be regarded as sufficiently approximating a perfect unidimensional scale. The most important of these is the coefficient of reproducibility (the proportion of item responses that can be correctly predicted from knowledge of the scale scores of respondents). A coefficient of reproducibility of .90 or more has become the standard criterion for determining if the reproducibility coefficient is sufficient to form a scale. [5]

While scale analysis has been severely criticized and is considered to be a less refined technique than factor analysis, it has been widely employed in the scaling of attitudes. This researcher selected this model for scaling because of the nature of responses and the items used as indicators of neighborhood satisfaction. In the analysis, a coefficient of reproducibility of .921 was obtained. This was considered sufficient to meet the standards mentioned earlier.

Dependent Variables

Research is usually aimed at identifying variables that are significantly related to or explain sociological phenomena. For classificatory purposes, the object of the investigation is frequently referred to as the dependent variable. In this research, the dependent variable is social adjustment. However, because of the complexity of the concept and inconsistencies in its use, two related approaches are used to measure the general social adjustment of the respondents and dimensions of social adjustment. The dimensions of social adjustment considered here are anomie, powerlessness, and social isolation. It is apparent to the researcher that other

dimensions of social adjustment are present. However, because of
certain restrictions of the data, these dimensions are not included
in this research.

Social Adjustment

In an effort to obtain a general index of social adjustment, a
twenty-six-item index was constructed. This index consists of the
following items:

1. Most people don't really care what happens to the next
fellow.

2. You sometimes can't help wondering whether anything is
worthwhile anymore.

3. Next to health, money is the most important thing in life.

4. No one really understands me.

5. To make money, there are no right and wrong ways any more,
only easy ways and hard ways.

6. I worry about the future facing today's children.

7. Sometimes I have the feeling other people are using me.

8. It is frightening to be responsible for the development of a
little child.

9. There is little or nothing I can do towards preventing a major
"shooting war."

10. There are so many decisions that have to be made today
that sometimes I could just "blow up."

11. There is little chance for promotion on the job unless a
man gets a break.

12. We're so regimented today that there's not much room for
choice even in personal matters.

13. We are just so many cogs in the machinery of life.

14. The future looks very dismal.

15. Sometimes I feel all alone in the world.

16. I don't get invited out by friends as often as I'd like.

17. Most people today seldom feel lonely.

18. Real friends are as easy as ever to find.

19. One can always find friends if he shows himself friendly.

20. The world in which we live is basically a friendly place.

21. There are few dependable ties between people anymore.

22. People are just naturally friendly and helpful.

23. I don't get to visit friends as often as I'd like.

24. Religion is mainly a myth.

25. I think single life is better than married life.

26. Human life is an expression of divine purpose.

Respondents were asked to agree or disagree with these statements and were assigned a score of 1 if the response logically indicated poor social adjustment, and a score of 2 if the response indicated an attitude compatible with the more generally accepted norms of society. Thus, a minimum score of 26 indicated that the respondent is not socially adjusted while a maximum score of 52 is an indication that the respondent is well adjusted. Obviously, several items are better indicants of social adjustment than others. A more reliable measuring instrument conceivably would assign differential weights to the items. It is for this reason that an effort is made in this study to identify dimensions of social adjustment and use a technique frequently used to measure the internal consistency of items.

Anomie, Powerlessness, and Social Isolation

It is logical to assume that an alienated individual is not socially adjusted to his specific social system. Therefore, it is necessary to isolate dimensions of alienation and/or social adjustment. These dimensions are anomie, social isolation, and powerlessness.

The items used to measure anomie were developed by Leo Srole; those used to measure powerlessness and social isolation were developed by Dean. The Guttman technique was used and a coefficient of reproducibility of .90 was obtained on all three scales. This coefficient is considered to be of sufficient magnitude to justify use of the scale to indicate the degree of social adjustment as measured by these three dimensions.

In an attempt to determine the relative degree of independence among the three scales and social adjustment, zero-order correlations were computed. The correlation matrix shown in Table 3 points to the interrelatedness and, to some extent, the independence of the dimensions.

In the matrix, anomie is highly correlated with total social adjustment score and powerlessness, while indicating a weak association with social isolation. The feeling of powerlessness follows the same pattern; that is, a very strong association exists between powerlessness and social adjustment, while a weak relationship exists between powerlessness and social isolation. In each case, the dimension of social adjustment is highly correlated with total social adjustment score. The strongest association is between anomie and social adjustment, followed by powerlessness and social isolation. The correlations indicate that the three dimensions are not independent and that there is some overlap between anomie and powerlessness. Because of the population studied in this research, these findings were anticipated. No attempt is made to establish a causal sequence among the three dependent variables. Also, these findings are consistent with other attempts to isolate the dimensions of social adjustment.

ANALYTICAL PROCEDURES

A special emphasis in this study concerns a discussion of the analytical procedures, because the techniques are somewhat involved and depart from the more usual methods employed in sociological research.[6] A category of multivaried procedures that have been designed especially for attribute data is used. The procedures allow one to rank the effects of selected independent variables on a designated dependent variable and compare the effects of different combinations of the various independent variables.[7] This technique is in many ways similar to the common multiple regression procedures for higher levels of measurement. The remainder of this chapter is devoted to a step-by-step discussion of the plan of analysis.

Phase I: Testing the Original Hypothesis

The first analytical operation involves the computation of simple frequency distributions, where each independent variable is cross-tabulated with each dependent variable. In this research, the

TABLE 3

Correlation Matrix for Dependent Variables

	A	SI	P	SA
A	1.00	.20	.67	.84
SI		1.00	.11	.41
P			1.00	.81
SA				1.00

A + anomie; SI = social isolation; P = powerlessness;
SA = social adjustment

dependent variable is social adjustment; however, dimensions of
social adjustment are considered. These dimensions are anomie,
powerlessness, and social isolation. These relationships are presented in tabular form and a chi-square test of statistical significance
is applied to determine if a significant relationship is observable for
the data.[8] Cramer's measure of association (V) is computed to
measure the strength of the relationship.[9] The V statistic is an index
of association utilizing chi-square values.

The purpose of this phase of the analysis is to partially re-
plicate studies that have examined the relationship between the independent and dependent variables. This phase, then, offers empirical
support for the hypothesized relationships.

Phase II: Computation of Subclass Proportions

Each dependent variable is redefined in terms of a high and low
state; that is, each variable is measured dichotomously using the
median as the criterion. The determination of whether a given variable is in a high or low state depends on either theory or previous
research. In studies of the relationship between tenure and social
adjustment, for example, homeowners live in higher quality housing
and should be more adequately socially adjusted. Thus, home ownership would be considered in a high state and renter status would be
in a low state of the tenure variable. In a similar manner, high
neighborhood satisfaction and high social participation are considered
to be in high states of their respective variables.

A complex frequency distribution is carried out controlling on the three independent variables. If we control on $\underline{m}$ dichotomous variables, $2\underline{m}$ observations result on the dependent variables. Thus, the three independent variables used here yield eight subclass observations. The subclass observations are presented in the form of the proportion of respondents in high states of the dependent variable. Table 4 reveals the variable configuration for each subclass.

Phase III: Partitioning of Variable Effects

The third stage of the analysis partitions the effects of each independent variable on the dependent variable when the other independent variables are controlled. In general, Coleman's approach to

TABLE 4

Control Table, with Proportions
for Different Variable Configurations

X(1) Tenure Status[a]	X(2) Social Participation[a]	X(3) Neighborhood Satisfaction[a]	Observed Proportions[b]
H	HSP	HNS	P(123)
H	HSP	LNS	$\bar{P}$(12)
H	LSP	HNS	$\bar{P}$(13)
H	LSP	LNS	$\bar{P}$(1)
R	HSP	HNS	$\bar{P}$(23)
R	HSP	LNS	$\bar{P}$(2)
R	LSP	HNS	$\bar{P}$(3)
R	LSP	LNS	$\bar{P}$(*)

[a]H = Home owner; R = Renter; HNS = High neighborhood satisfaction; LNS = Low neighborhood satisfaction; HSP = High social participation; LSP = Low social participation.

[b]The notation used for identifying proportions is such that the numbers in parentheses refer to each of the independent variables; a number for a particular variable appears when that variable is in high state. P(123) refers to that subclass where tenure status, neighborhood satisfaction, and social participation are in a high state. P(12) refers to the subclass where tenure status and neighborhood satisfaction are in a high state and social participation in a low state. P(*) refers to the subclass where all variables are in a low state.

estimating variable effects is based on averages of differences in
proportions between subclasses in which the independent variable
is in a high state and the condition in which it is in a low state. The
mathematical derivation of Coleman's formulas is based on the method
of least squares. The general equation for $\underline{m}$ dichotomous independent
variables is presented in this manner:

> If there are m independent attributes altogether, then
> there are, altogether $2^{\underline{m}}p$'s. For any attribute, there
> are, therefore, half this many pairs, $2^{\underline{m}-1}$, to be aver-
> aged. If the index $\underline{C}$ signifies a particular combination
> of the other dichotomies (e.g., state 1 on attributes 2, 3,
> 5, 8, $\underline{m}$, and state 0 on all others, exluding the one in
> question), then there are $2^{\underline{m}-1}$ such combinations, and
> the proportion of difference for each combination is $P_{\underline{ic}}-P_{\underline{c}}$.
> The equations for the effects of attribute $\underline{i}$ are:

$$\underline{a_i} = \frac{1}{2\underline{m}-1} \qquad\qquad \sum_{\underline{C}\ =\ 1}^{2^{\underline{m}-1}} (P_{\underline{ic}}-P_{\underline{c}})$$

or if we let $2\underline{m}-1 = \underline{V}$,

$$\underline{a_i} = \frac{1}{\underline{V}} \qquad\qquad \sum_{\underline{V_c}\ =\ 1}^{\underline{V}} (P_{\underline{ic}}-P_{\underline{c}})$$

For two independent attributes, there are two comparisons on each; for three, there are four comparisons; for four, eight comparisons; and so on. [10]

When this general equation is applied to the three model cases,
the following set of computation formulas can be derived. The computational procedure is to divide the sum of subclass proportions
where the particular variable is in a high state minus the condition
where the particular variable is in a low state by $2\underline{m}-1$.

For computing the effects of $\underline{X}(1)$, $\underline{X}(2)$, and $\underline{X}(3)$, the following
procedure is used:

Effect of $\underline{X}(1)$

$$\underline{A}_{1=\frac{1}{2}}^{2}\ [\ \underline{P}(123)-\underline{P}(23)+\underline{P}(12)-\underline{P}(2)+\underline{P}(13)-\underline{P}(3)+\underline{P}(1)-\underline{P}(*)\ ]$$

Effect of $\underline{X}(2)$

$$\underline{A}_{2=\frac{1}{2}}{}^2 \left[\underline{P}(123)-\underline{P}(13)+\underline{P}(12)-\underline{P}(1)+\underline{P}(23)-\underline{P}(3)+\underline{P}(2)-\underline{P}(*) \right]$$

Effect of X(3)

$$\underline{A}_{3=\frac{1}{2}}{}^2 \left[\underline{P}(123)-\underline{P}(12)+\underline{P}(13)-\underline{P}(1)+\underline{P}(23)-\underline{P}(2)+\underline{P}(3)-\underline{P}(*) \right]$$

Coleman refers to the residual effect as random shock. Random shock is a measure of the unexplained variance observed in the sub-class proportions. Furthermore, random shock can be partitioned into two sources: (1) random shock in the direction of higher subclass proportions; and (2) random shock in the direction of lower subclass proportions. The formulas for these secondary random shock effects are lengthy and are omitted. [11] Random shock is computationally defined as:

$$\underline{RS} = 1 - \text{effects of } \underline{X}(1) + \text{effects of } \underline{X}(2) \text{ and effects of } \underline{X}(3)$$

A final measure of composite effect can easily be computed:

$$\text{Composite Effect} = \sum_{i=1}^{m} \underline{ai}$$

$$\text{Also} \sum \underline{ai} + \underline{RS} = 1$$

Thus, composite effect $= 1 - \underline{RS}$

The composite effect coefficient is perhaps the most useful of effect measures because it is an index of the explanatory power of the entire model. Also, the composite effect coefficient can be used to compare the explanatory power of one model with another; for example, home ownership may explain more variance in anomie than in powerlessness or social isolation.

Phase IV: Test of Statistical Significance
for Effect Measures

Following the computation of estimates of the various effects on the dependent variable, it is desirable that the statistical significance of each effect estimate be evaluated. The following ratio can be tested by using a standardized cumulative normal distribution. [12]

$$U_1 = \frac{\text{Effect Estimate } - \text{ Zero}}{\text{Standard Deviation of Effect Estimate}}$$

Coleman's method of computation of the standard deviation of the effect estimate is based on a pooling of the various subclass proportion variances where

$$\text{Each Subclass Variance} = \underline{P}j(1-\underline{P}j)/nj$$

The pooled variance is made by cumulating the subclass variances and dividing by 2^{2m-2}.

Phase V: Model Evaluation

Although tests of significance were used to determine the relevance of the effects of each variable in each model, it is also necessary to evaluate the observed proportions in relation to the theoretical or expected proportions in each model. The procedure permits the researcher to determine the "goodness of fit" of a given model. The deviations of the observed proportions from the theoretical expectancy can be obtained from the procedure in Table 5. The most important concern here is with the magnitude and direction of the deviations.

Finally, to reiterate, this model yields an estimate of the variance in the dependent variable that can be attributed to each independent

TABLE 5

Procedure for Estimating Parameters for Three Variable Models[a]

$\underline{P}*()$	=					+	$\underline{r}$
$\underline{P}*(1)$	=	$\underline{a}(1)$				+	$\underline{r}$
$\underline{P}*(2)$	=		+	$\underline{a}(2)$		+	$\underline{r}$
$\underline{P}*(12)$	=	$\underline{a}(1)$	+	$\underline{a}(2)$		+	$\underline{r}$
$\underline{P}*(3)$	=				+ $\underline{a}(3)$	+	$\underline{r}$
$\underline{P}*(13)$	=	$\underline{a}(1)$			+ $\underline{a}(3)$	+	$\underline{r}$
$\underline{P}*(23)$	=			$\underline{a}(2)$	+ $\underline{a}(3)$	+	$\underline{r}$
$\underline{P}*(123)$	=	$\underline{a}(1)$	+	$\underline{a}(2)$	+ $\underline{a}(3)$	+	$\underline{r}$

[a]The numbers in parentheses refer to the independent variables. See Table 4, p. 71.

variable. Thus, it is possible to evaluate the effect each independent variable has on the dependent variable. In this research, the aim is to evaluate the effect of three independent variables on social adjustment.

SUMMARY

This chapter was concerned with a general description of the housing conditions in the area of the study. Attention was focused on the sampling procedures and operationalization of major concepts. The final section of this chapter was devoted to a discussion of the analytical procedures. Chapter 5 is concerned with the analysis of the data.

NOTES

1. Lewis Killian and Charles M. Grigg, "A Study of Community Problems and the Role of the Bi-Racial Committee in a Southern City" (Institute for Social Research, Florida State University, 1961).

2. See William H. Sewell, The Construction and Standardization of a Scale for the Measurement of the Socio-Economic Status of Oklahoma Farm Families, Oklahoma A & M Agricultural Experiment Station Technical Bulletin No. 9 (April, 1940).

3. Claire Selltiz et al., Research Methods in Social Relations (New York: Holt, Rhinehart and Winston, 1964), p. 344.

4. Ernest R. Hilgard, Introduction to Psychology (New York: Harcourt, Brace & World, 1962), p. 565.

5. Louis Guttman, "A Basis for Scaling Qualitative Data," American Sociological Review, IX (April, 1944), 139-150; idem, "The Cornell Technique for Scale and Intensity Analysis," Educational and Psychological Measurement, VII (Summer, 1947), 247-79.

6. This discussion is based primarily on a report prepared by Arthur Cosby for a statistics class conducted by the author.

7. Coleman discusses the logic in mathematical derivation of a multivaried approach to attribute data in his text on mathematical sociology; see James S. Coleman, Introduction to Mathematical Sociology (New York: Free Press, 1964), pp. 189-240.

8. H. M. Blalock, Jr., Social Statistics (New York: McGraw-Hill, 1960), pp. 212-21.

9. Ibid., pp. 225-28.

10. Coleman, op. cit., p. 200.

11. For a discussion of the computational procedures, see ibid., pp. 200-01.

12. Coleman's method of testing the significance of effect estimates is based on the known distributions of the difference between proportions; see ibid., pp. 205-209.

INTRODUCTION

This chapter is concerned with testing the theoretical propositions. Also, by the application of Coleman's model for the analysis
of attribute data, an estimate of variance in the dependent variables
is included.

RELATIONSHIP BETWEEN TENURE AND
HOUSING QUALITY

Although change in tenure does not necessarily result in an
improvement in the quality of the housing environment, in this study
the fact that all the respondents previously lived in the black ghetto
of the metropolitan community caused the change in residence among
all respondents to result in improved housing conditions.[1] However,
it is hypothesized that the respondents whose tenure changed from
renter to owner experienced a significantly greater improvement in
housing quality.

Table 6 shows the relationship between tenure and eight subjective
measures of housing quality.[2] As anticipated, the data indicate a
significant gain in the quality of housing. A close inspection of the
data contained in Tables 1 through 8 in Appendix B reveals the following
information: (1) Only 3.7 percent of the new homeowners were dissatisfied with the amount of air and sunlight, compared to 13.4 percent
of the renters; (2) 11.6 percent of the owners were dissatisfied with
street noise, compared with 22.9 percent of the renters; (3) 24.3
percent of the homeowners were dissatisfied with heating and cooling
equipment, compared to 38.6 percent of the renters; (4) 18.4 percent
of the owners were dissatisfied with the amount of room, compared

TABLE 6

Summary of the Relationship between Tenure and Quality
of the Housing Environment Using the $\chi2$ Distribution.

	$\underline{X}_1$	$\underline{X}_2$	$\underline{X}_3$	$\underline{X}_4$
Tenure	9.41*	9.62*	14.43**	53.64**

	$\underline{X}_5$	$\underline{X}_6$	$\underline{X}_7$	$\underline{X}_8$
Tenure	22.36**	55.62**	47.23**	30.83**

$\underline{N}$ = 439   * = $\underline{Pr}$ <.01   ** = $\underline{Pr}$ <.001

X_1 = Heating (cooling) equipment
$\overline{X}_2$ = Amount of street noise
$\overline{X}_3$ = Amount of air and sunlight
$\overline{X}_4$ = Amount of open space around house
X_5 = Amount of room
$\overline{X}_6$ = Attitude toward residence
$\overline{X}_7$ = Amount of closet space
$\overline{X}_8$ = Amount of privacy

TABLE 7

Summary of the Relationship between Tenure and Quality
of the Housing Environment, Using Cramer's $\underline{V}$ for
Association with Same Variable Designation

	$\underline{X}_1$	$\underline{X}_2$	$\underline{X}_3$	$\underline{X}_4$	$\underline{X}_5$	$\underline{X}_6$	$\underline{X}_7$	$\underline{X}_8$
Tenure	.15	.15	.18	.35	.22	.35	.32	.26

to 39.3 percent of the renters; (5) 3.2 percent of the owners were
dissatisfied with the amount of open space around the house, compared
to 26.0 percent of the renters; (6) 8.7 percent of the owners were
dissatisfied with the amount of privacy, compared to 28.9 percent of
the renters; (7) 19.5 percent of the owners were dissatisfied with the
amount of closet space, compared to 51.5 percent of the renters; and
(8) only 5.3 percent of the new homeowners were generally dissatisfied
with their new residence, compared to 30.9 percent of the renters.

These data offer additional support for the hypotheses to be
tested later. The strengths of the relationships are measured by

Cramer's V. The strongest relationships are found between tenure
and variables X_4, X_5, X_6, X_7, and X_8. Also, these variables—open
space, room, residence, closet space, and privacy—are considered
the most important in other studies concerned with social psychological
consequences of housing quality.

PROPOSITION I: There is a positive relationship between
tenure and social adjustment.

In the previous section of this chapter, it was established that
change in tenure resulted in an improvement in the quality of the housing environment for the respondents in this study. Invariably, the
respondents who previously resided in slum areas of the city and moved
to the suburbs while changing their status from renter to homeowner
experienced a significantly greater improvement in housing quality.

Another assumption made in this research is that home ownership is one of the most valued goals among lower-class Americans.
In this study, a large proportion of the persons displaced by the expressway authority were given an opportunity to become home buyers
and took advantage of this opportunity. As a result, the normative
orientation of the home buyers toward society should be affected.

As the literature and theoretical frame suggest, then, the change
in tenure should logically result in a change in attitudes that are
indicative of the degree the respondents are socially adjusted. As
stated previously, social adjustment is operationalized in the form
of twenty-six items purporting to measure several dimensions of the
normative orientation of the respondents. Each item was given equal
weight. Thus the range of possible scores in 26 to 52. Scale scores
between 39 and 52 indicate adequate social adjustment. The median
was used in dichotomizing the respondents.[3] Data contained in Table
8 offer tentative support for the proposition.

In Chapter 3 the theoretical propositions predicted that change
in tenure from renter to owner would result in an accumulated social
adjustment score significantly higher than those of respondents moving
from one ghetto to another and retaining the status of renter, and,
thus, not significantly improving their housing quality. The data
contained in Table 8 support this proposition. A higher percentage
of the owners have accumulated social adjustment scores above 38.
In fact, 60.7 percent of the owners fall in this range, while only
46.6 percent of the renters indicate satisfactory adjustment to their
social environment. It should be noted that the relationship is not as
strong as anticipated. However, in this measure of social adjustment,
several dimensions are involved. Subsequent analysis in this chapter
will attempt to isolate these dimensions and shed some light on the
relationship as depicted in the above table.

TABLE 8

Relationship between Tenure and Social
Adjustment

	Owner		Renter	
	Number	Percent	Number	Percent
S1*	187	60. 7	61	46. 6
S2*	121	39. 3	70	53. 4
Total	308	100. 0	131	100. 0

S1* = Social adjustment scale scores from 39 to 52.
S2* = Social adjustment scale scores from 26 to 38.

χ^2 = 7. 49   Pr < 01   V = . 13

PROPOSITION II: Change in tenure is related to the degree
of social participation; home owners are expected to participate more frequently than renters.

One of the most frequently mentioned hypotheses concerning
home ownership is the increased involvement and frequency of interaction that usually follow. However, this proposition is generally
more applicable to middle-class white Americans. In the present
context, since the respondents were previously ghetto-dwelling blacks
in a metropolitan area, it was hypothesized that the upward mobility
commonly associated with change in tenure to home owner would be
felt by the respondents and would result in a higher degree of participation in community affairs. The Chapin social participation scale
was used. Scale scores of 0 were classified as inactive; scores from
1 to 10 were classified as rarely active, and scores above 10 were
classified as active. Table 9 shows the relationship between tenure
and social participation.

The data support the proposition that more homeowners participate in voluntary associations than do renters. In fact, over one-half
of the homeowners participate in voluntary associations while less
than one-fourth of the renters participate. Since the majority of the
respondents in the total sample are low-income, poorly educated
blacks, it is feasible to assume that the newly acquired status of homeowner has served as a stimulus for more active participation in local

TABLE 9

Relationship between Tenure and Social Participation

Social Participation	Owner		Renter	
	Number	Percent	Number	Percent
Inactive	152	49. 4	100	76. 3
Rarely Active	93	30. 2	20	15. 3
Active	63	20. 4	11	8. 4
Total	308	100. 0	131	100. 0

$\underline{N} = 439$ $\chi^2 = 27.53$ $\underline{Pr} < .001$ $\underline{V} = .25$

community affairs. There is also the interpretation that the respondents residing in each of the five suburban housing developments found it necessary to participate more frequently in order to protect their vested interests in the community.

PROPOSITION III: Tenure is related to the degree of neighborhood satisfaction; more specifically, home owners will indicate a greater degree of satisfaction with their neighborhood than will renters.

The forced displacement of a high proportion of the respondents resulted in a move from the ghetto section of the central city to newly developed suburbs, while a significant number moved to an adjacent ghetto. For those who experienced a move to the suburb and, subsequently, single dwelling units, it was anticipated that there would emerge a sense of neighborliness and greater satisfaction with the physical environment as well as with services in the neighborhood. It has previously been established that homeowners are definitely more satisfied with the physical aspects of their recently acquired homes. In measuring neighborhood satisfaction, a Guttman scale was developed. The range of scores was from 5 to 15. The median was used to dichotomize the respondents into categories indicating satisfaction and dissatisfaction with the neighborhood. Table 10 assesses the relationship between tenure and neighborhood satisfaction.

The analysis of the relationship offers tentative support for the original proposition. However, the relationship as measured by

TABLE 10

Relationship between Tenure and Neighborhood Satisfaction

| Neighborhood Satisfaction | Tenure | | | |
| | Owner | | Renter | |
	Number	Percent	Number	Percent
Satisfied	122	39. 6	40	30. 5
Dissatisfied	186	60. 4	91	69. 5
Total	308	100. 0	131	100. 0

N = 439 χ^2 = 3. 26   Pr < 05   V = .09

Cramer's V is not as strong as anticipated. Surprisingly, only 39. 6 percent of the owners were classified as being satisfied with their neighborhood. A much higher proportion was expected.

Inspection of the items contained in the satisfaction scale reveals that one item pertains to attitudes toward police protection. Almost invariably, the respondents were negative in their attitudes toward police protection—for which homeowners had to pay. This dissatisfaction with the police was expressed during the interview sessions. Thus, the move, regardless of whether it entailed going to a suburb or adjacent ghetto, did not alter the black's perception of police protection. This, too, perhaps explains why a small proportion of both groups indicated satisfaction with all five areas of neighborhood life measured by the scale.

PROPOSITION IV: Social participation is related to the degree of social adjustment; that is, the more frequently one participates in the voluntary associations in the community, the higher his adjustment score.

Proposition IV has previously been found to be true among almost all strata of the population. However, when this proposition was supported in previous research, especially research concerned with black Americans, the emphasis did not include other possible consequences for the general normative orientation to society. The assumption here is that the degree of social adjustment is largely determined by relations of individuals with each other and by their membership in groups. Thus, social participation serves as an integrative mechanism for individuals and society.

TABLE 11

Relationship between Social Participation and Social
Adjustment

	Inactive		Rarely Active		Active	
	Number	Percent	Number	Percent	Number	Percent
S1	140	55.6	58	51.3	50	67.6
S2	112	44.4	55	48.7	24	32.4
Total	252	100.0	113	100.0	74	100.0

N = 439 χ^2 = 5.02   Pr < .05   V =   V = .11

The data presented in Table 11 support the original proposition.
A close inspection of the findings indicates that 67.6 percent of those
persons active in voluntary associations scored high on social adjustment, while only 55.6 percent of the inactives scored high on social
adjustment. More interesting, however, is the distribution in the
rarely active category. This unanticipated distribution might be
explained by the fact that probably at no other time in history have
the blacks been more self-conscious. Therefore, when we talk about
social participation reinforcing favorable attitudes toward one's
environment, we must be careful to look at the problem in this new
context. Perhaps the most crucial variable to be considered today
would be the type of voluntary association in which the black participates. If the association is an extremely militant organization,
then increased social participation could possibly have the opposite
effect as predicted by consensus theorists.

> PROPOSITION V: Neighborhood satisfaction is related to
> the degree of social adjustment; more specifically, the
> more satisfied one is with his local neighborhood, the
> higher his social adjustment score.

Previous research has pointed out the relationship between
contentment with one's community or neighborhood and social adjustment. This relationship is presented in Table 12.

The data do not support the research proposition. Among the
persons satisfied with their neighborhood, 53.7 percent scored high
on social adjustment. Actually, a slightly higher proportion of

TABLE 12

Relationship between Neighborhood Satisfaction and
Social Adjustment

| Social | Neighborhood Satisfaction | | | |
| | Satisfied | | Dissatisfied | |
Adjustment	Number	Percent	Number	Percent
$\underline{S}1$	87	53.7	161	58.1
$\underline{S}2$	75	46.3	116	41.9
Total	162	100.0	277	100.0

$\underline{N}$ = 439 χ^2 = .81   Pr < .50

persons dissatisfied with their neighborhood reflected adequate social
adjustment. Again, it appears that dissatisfaction is the modal
response pattern. An elaboration on the apparent independence of
the two variables is presented in the following section.

In sum, it is noted that four of the five propositions were supported by the data. Also, it is noted that eight subjective measures
of housing quality were significantly related to tenure. At this stage
in the analysis, it is necessary to evaluate the total effects of the
independent criterion on social adjustment.

MODEL I: Multivariate Analysis of the Effects of Independent Criterion on Social Adjustment

Following the analysis of the simple relationship between tenure,
social participation, and neighborhood satisfaction to social adjustment, a multivariate analysis was introduced. It should be noted that
each of the simple relationships was significant and in the direction
predicted by the research hypothesis. However, before introducing
the multivariate model suggested by Coleman for the analysis of
attribute data, it is necessary to define each independent variable in
terms of its relationship to the social adjustment. Variable delineation
is contained in Table 13.

The criteria for the dichotomous classification of respondents
into high and low states is based on a theoretical understanding of
the implications of tenure, social participation, and neighborhood
satisfaction for individual social adjustment. For example, home

TABLE 13

Definition of High and Low States of Three
Independent Variables

Variable[a]	High State	Low State
Tenure	Owner	Renter
Social Participation	Participants	Nonparticipants
Neighborhood Satisfaction	Satisfaction	Dissatisfaction

[a]A discussion of the operationalization of these variables can be found in Chapter 4.

ownership, one of the most important success symbols in America, especially for low-income blacks, is positively related to social adjustment and, consequently, categorized in a high state of tenure. In a similar manner, social participation and neighborhood satisfaction were categorized in high states. Table 14 contains the variable configuration for social adjustment.

At this stage in the analysis, it is necessary to partition the effects of each independent variable on the dependent variable while the effects of the other independent variables are controlled. Table 15 gives the effect estimate for each independent variable and the corresponding tests of statistical significance (computational tables are found in Appendix B).

The effect estimates show the relative size of the partial relationship of tenure, social participation, and neighborhood satisfaction to social adjustment. The analysis indicates that tenure explained a significant portion of the variation in social adjustment, while social participation explained the least. An interesting finding is the significant inverse relationship between neighborhood satisfaction and social adjustment. A partial explanation for this relationship can be obtained from the data contained in Table 14. Observation of the subclass proportions indicates that a high proportion of the renters (87.5 percent) scored low on adjustment but high on social participation and neighborhood satisfaction. Thus the relationship between social participation and adjustment, and the relationship between neighborhood satisfaction and adjustment, are in the opposite direction from the theoretical expectancy. The fact that only eight cases fell in this subclass could account for the deviation.

TABLE 14

Proportions of Respondents with Low Social Adjustment
for Different Variable Configurations for Three
Independent Variables

Tenure	Social Participation	Neighborhood	Observed Proportion	Number
Homeowner	Participant	Satisfied	.41	54
Homeowner	Participant	Dissatisfied	.40	102
Homeowner	Nonparticipant	Satisfied	.40	68
Homeowner	Nonparticipant	Dissatisfied	.37	84
Renter	Participant	Satisfied	.88	8
Renter	Participant	Dissatisfied	.39	23
Renter	Nonparticipant	Satisfied	.59	32
Renter	Nonparticipant	Dissatisfied	.52	68

TABLE 15

Comparison of Variable Effect Estimates for the
Independent Variables on Social Adjustment

Variable	Effect Estimate	Z Statistic[a]	Statistical Significance
Tenure	.20	3.65	Pr < .0001
Social Participation	-.05	.92	Pr = .1788
Neighborhood Satisfaction	-.15	2.73	Pr < .0032

[a]The normal distribution was used to determine the probabilities
associated with effect estimates.

MODEL II: Multivariate Analysis of the Effects of Independent Criterion on Powerlessness

In the earlier discussion of social adjustment, it was assumed
that there are several dimensions to the degree individuals internalize
normative orientations to society. One dimension identified in the
research and previous studies is powerlessness. This social-psychological state of the individual refers to the expectancy or probability
held by the individual that his own behavior cannot determine the
occurrence of the outcomes or reinforcements he seeks. A five-item
Guttman scale was used to determine the degree of powerlessness
experienced by the individuals in the sample. The arithmetic mean
was used to dichotomize response patterns. Tables 16 and 17 contain
the variable configurations for powerlessness and the effect estimates.

The estimate of the effect of each of the independent variables
on the degree of powerlessness points out that all three variables
explain essentially an equal amount of the variation in the dependent
variable.

However, as in the model concerning social adjustment, neighborhood satisfaction, and social participation have an effect opposite
from the hypothesized relationship. Again, it is the unusual finding
contained in the subclass of renters who participate frequently and
are relatively content with their neighborhood. As mentioned previously, invariably the move from the slum area of the city demolished
in order to construct an expressway resulted in improved quality of
housing. Thus, apparently the renters, especially those participating
in voluntary associations, perceived their move to adjacent slums as
an improvement and subsequently, showed this in their response to
items intended to measure satisfaction with the neighborhood. Perhaps more important is the 11.9 percent of the variation explained
by tenure. Here we find that 40.7 percent of the home owners who
participate in voluntary associations and who indicate satisfaction
with their neighborhood indicate a high degree of powerlessness. A
more careful analysis of the contents of Table 16 reveals that only
34.5 percent of this group, although nonparticipants and dissatisfied,
show a high degree of powerlessness. This observation suggests that
neither social participation nor neighborhood satisfaction is operating
positively in the individual definition of the objective situation that
includes his expectancy of control over certain events as measured
by the items contained in the scale developed to measure powerlessness.

MODEL III: Multivariate Analysis of the Effects of the
Independent Criterion on Social Isolation

TABLE 16

Proportions of Respondents Indicating a High Degree of
Powerlessness for Different Variable Configurations
for Three Independent Variables

Tenure	Social Participation	Neighborhood Satisfaction	Proportion	Number
Homeowner	Participant	Satisfied	.41	54
Homeowner	Participant	Dissatisfied	.47	102
Homeowner	Nonparticipant	Satisfied	.38	68
Homeowner	Nonparticipant	Dissatisfied	.35	84
Renter	Participant	Satisfied	.88	8
Renter	Participant	Dissatisfied	.35	23
Renter	Nonparticipant	Satisfied	.41	32
Renter	Nonparticipant	Dissatisfied	.46	68

TABLE 17

Comparison of Variable Effect Estimates for the
Independent Variables on Powerlessness

Variable	Effect Estimate	Z Statistic	Statistical Significance
Tenure	.12	2.19	$\underline{Pr}$ = .0143
Social Participation	-.13	2.34	$\underline{Pr}$ = .0096
Neighborhood Satisfaction	-.11	2.06	$\underline{Pr}$ = .0197

In a previous section of this research, social isolation was identified as one of the more important dimensions of alienation and, thus, important in the conceptual approach to understanding the dynamics of the social effects of the housing environment on individual social adjustment. Social isolation generally refers to the efforts or lack of effort on the part of the individual to establish and maintain relationships with other members of society. An elaboration of this basic notion is that social isolationists tend to assign low reward value to goals and beliefs that are typically highly valued in a given society. Thus it is logical to postulate that home ownership, social participation, and neighborhood contentment would be inversely related to the degree of social isolation as measured by the five-item Guttman scale presented in Chapter 5. Since the use of Coleman's attribute model necessitates a dichotomous classification, the arithmetic mean was used. Tables 18 and 19 represent the variable configuration for analyzing the effects of the three independent variables on social isolation.

The analysis of variable effects on social isolation did not prove to be statistically significant, although the composite effect of tenure and social participation explains 15 percent of the variation. As one would suspect, social participation explains the largest portion of the variation. A close inspection of the observed proportions contained in Table 18 reveals that renters who do not participate in voluntary associations but are satisfied with their neighborhood are the most isolated group. In this subclass, 84.4 percent are considered to be socially isolated. A possible explanation for the apparent isolation of this group is the condition generally associated with the urban way of life. That is, for some urban dwellers there is a tendency to indicate relative satisfaction, or perhaps, and more appropriately for this sample, resignation to their station in life and a preference for little interaction with others.

MODEL IV: Multivariate Analysis of the Effects of the Independent Criterion on Anomie

The final dimension of social adjustment considered in the analysis is anomie. That anomie is important in viewing social adjustment is evident by the volumes of research and theory on the subject. Much of the research has conceptualized anomie as resulting from lack of opportunity to realize the more important socially approved goals in society. Thus, when individuals in a success-oriented society such as ours do not have the available means to achieve these goals, the resulting social-psychological reaction is anomie. According to this approach, low-income blacks in a metropolitan area are the most unlikely group in American society to experience upward mobility and consequently, by definition, are the most anomic stratum in America.

TABLE 18

Proportions of Respondents Indicating a High Degree of
Social Isolation for Different Variable Configurations
for Three Independent Variables

Tenure	Social Participation	Neighborhood Satisfaction	Observed Proportion	Number
Homeowner	Participant	Satisfied	.65	54
Homeowner	Participant	Dissatisfied	.51	102
Homeowner	Nonparticipant	Satisfied	.46	68
Homeowner	Nonparticipant	Dissatisfied	.58	84
Renter	Participant	Satisfied	.50	8
Renter	Participant	Dissatisfied	.52	23
Renter	Nonparticipant	Satisfied	.84	32
Renter	Nonparticipant	Dissatisfied	.62	68

TABLE 19

Comparison of Variable Effect Estimates for the
Independent Variables on Social Isolation

Variable	Effect Estimate	Z Statistic	Statistical Significance
Tenure	.07	1.15	$\underline{Pr}$ = .1251
Social Participation	.08	1.29	$\underline{Pr}$ = .0985
Neighborhood Satisfaction	-.05	.86	$\underline{Pr}$ = .1949

In this research, a large portion of the ghetto-dwelling, low-income blacks were given an opportunity to become home buyers and move to a new suburban housing development. The data contained in Tables 20 and 21 assess the effects of the change in tenure, as well as social participation and neighborhood satisfaction, on anomie. In the measurement of anomie, the usual five-item Srole scale was used. The arithmetic mean was the criterion for determining high and low states of anomie.

In partitioning the variable effects of each of the independent variables and summing to obtain the composite effect, only 11 percent of the variation in anomie can be attributed to all three independent variables. However, no independent variable explained a significant portion of the variation in anomie. This finding is contrary to the hypotheses set forth in Chapter 3. Inspection of the subclass proportions shows that almost 54 percent of the homeowners who participate in voluntary associations and are also satisfied with their neighborhood are anomic. Theoretically, this subclass should be the least anomic of all. However, the least anomic are homeowners who do not participate in voluntary associations and are dissatisfied with their neighborhood. Inspection of other subclasses (for example, renters who participate and are dissatisfied $\overline{\text{Pr}}$ = . 500) implies to this researcher that anomie is high among all subclasses of this sample. This finding, to some degree, supports the contention that high states of anomie are prevalent among low-income blacks in urban areas. The theoretical significance of this finding is that lack of opportunity in the social structure does not necessarily result in an intensified state of anomie. Elaborations on this finding are presented in Chapter 6.

EVALUATION OF MODELS AND ELABORATION

Model I

An evaluation of the estimate of the effects of each of the independent variables on social adjustment is necessary in order to determine how well the data fit the model. Table 22 compares the theoretical and observed proportions.

The actual data conform relatively well to the theoretical proportions with the exception of subclasses $\underline{P}$ (23) and $\underline{P}$ (2). In subclass P (23), the actual proportion of renters who participate and are satisfied with their neighborhood but are not adequately adjusted is . 875. The theoretical expectancy is . 693. This means that there are 18. 2 percent more in this subclass than would be expected. One explanation is the small number of cases (8) in this subclass. However, other factors outside the model could be operating to affect the

TABLE 20

Proportion of Respondents Indicating a High Degree of
Anomie for Different Variable Configurations for
Three Independent Variables

Tenure	Social Participation	Neighborhood Satisfaction	Observed Proportion	Number
Homeowner	Participant	Satisfied	.54	54
Homeowner	Participant	Dissatisfied	.68	102
Homeowner	Nonparticipant	Satisfied	.50	68
Homeowner	Nonparticipant	Dissatisfied	.49	84
Renter	Participant	Satisfied	.50	8
Renter	Participant	Dissatisfied	.61	23
Renter	Nonparticipant	Satisfied	.66	32
Renter	Nonparticipant	Dissatisfied	.63	68

TABLE 21

Comparison of Variable Effect Estimates for the
Independent Variables on Anomie

Variable	Effect Estimate	Z Statistic	Statistical Significance
Tenure	.05	.71	$Pr = .2389$
Social Participation	.01	.18	$Pr = .4286$
Neighborhood Satisfaction	.05	.83	$Pr = .2033$

TABLE 22

Comparison of Theoretical and Observed Proportions
for Model I

Variable Configuration[a]	Observed Proportion	Theoretical Proportion	Deviation
P (123)	.41	.49	-.08
P (12)	.40	.35	.05
P (13)	.40	.44	-.04
P (1)	.37	.29	.08
P (23)	.88	.69	.19
P (2)	.39	.54	-.15
P (3)	.59	.64	-.05
P*	.51	.49	.02

[a]Symbolic representations of variable configurations are the same as presented in Chapter 4.

interrelationship of the variables. In an attempt to elaborate on the original relationship, sex was introduced as a control variable. Computational tables using sex as a control are found in Appendix B. In these tables, we are primarily concerned with $P_i - P*$, which represents the deviations from the observed proportions.

Again, in evaluating Model I, the largest deviation occurred in subclass P (23). When sex is introduced as a control, 100 percent of the males in this subclass are not adequately adjusted, whereas 75 percent of the females indicate unsatisfactory adjustment. More interesting, however, is the deviation from the theoretical expectancy. The deviation among the females is .03, compared to .34 for the males. Thus, there appear to be factors operating among the males to affect the assumption of linearity. A possible explanation is that males are, for the most part, unadjusted. This is especially true for males who rent and are actively involved in voluntary associations.

The other major deviation in Model I is in the subclass P̲ (2). This subclass refers to renters who participate in voluntary associations but are dissatisfied with their neighborhood. The observed proportion low in social adjustment is .391. The theoretical expectancy is .544. Thus the deviation is -.153. This means that the relationship is in the opposite direction from the prediction. However, when sex is introduced in an effort to specify more clearly the nature of the relationship, we find that the model is more efficient for the females than the males. Among the females the deviation is -.017, while the deviation occurring in the male sample is -.303.

It should be noted that in the subclasses that deviate significantly from the observed proportions, the sample size was very small and that this factor alone could explain the deviations. Thus, with the exception of two subclasses [P̲ (23) and P̲ (2)] the model provides a good fit for the data.

Model II

Model II is concerned with the effect of tenure, social participation, and neighborhood satisfaction on a dimension of social adjustment referred to as powerlessness. Table 23 evaluates this model.

The comparison between theoretical and observed subclass proportions indicates that subclasses P̲ (23) and P̲ (2) show the greatest deviations. It is noted that these subclasses also showed the largest deviation in Model I. Again, to elaborate on the original model, sex was introduced as a control variable. An inspection of the subclass proportions with sex as a control yields the same conclusions as in Model I. It is among males that we find the greatest deviation.

The most relevant finding with sex as a control is the variation in powerlessness among males and females that can be attributed to the independent variables. Among males 15 percent of the variation is attributed to tenure while only 6 percent of the variation is explained among females. This finding points out the significance of home ownership for males, especially when it is related to a sense of powerlessness. Thus, the change in tenure appears to have had a more positive effect on the males.

In general, the model provides a good fit for the data. The subclasses with the greatest deviations are the same as in Model I. Sample size is one important consideration, as is the apparent effect social participation has had on the relationship between neighborhood satisfaction and a sense of powerlessness.

TABLE 23

Comparison of Theoretical and Observed Proportions
for Model II

Variable Configuration	Observed Proportions	Theoretical Proportions	Deviation
$\underline{P}$ (123)	.41	.51	-.10
$\underline{P}$ (12)	.47	.39	.08
$\underline{P}$ (13)	.38	.38	.00
$\underline{P}$ (1)	.35	.27	.08
$\underline{P}$ (23)	.88	.63	.25
$\underline{P}$ (2)	.35	.51	-.16
$\underline{P}$ (3)	.41	.50	-.09
$\underline{P}$*	.46	.39	.07

Model III

The analysis of the effects of tenure, social participation, and neighborhood satisfaction on social isolation was presented in Model III. The "goodness of fit" of this model is presented in Table 24.

An evaluation of the deviations from the theoretical proportions yields four subclasses with large deviations. These subclasses are P (123), P (13), P(23), and $\underline{P}$ (3). The introduction of sex as an additional control variable reveals that, in each subclass, the deviations among females are considerably higher than the deviations found among the males. There appears to be a tendency for a much higher proportion of females to be socially isolated than males in all subclasses of the independent variables. Also, the effect of tenure among females is -.0499, while among males the effect is estimated to be .1887. Thus, tenure tends to have a very positive effect on males, while the relationship is opposite among females. The conclusion is that the model is much more appropriate for males than for females in the total sample.

TABLE 24

Comparison of Theoretical and Observed Proportions
for Model III

Variable Configuration	Observed Proportions	Theoretical Proportions	Deviation
P (123)	.65	.54	.11
P (12)	.51	.48	.03
P (13)	.46	.62	.16
P (1)	.58	.56	.02
P (23)	.50	.61	-.11
P (2)	.52	.55	-.03
P (3)	.84	.69	.15
P*	.62	.63	-.01

Model IV

The data analyzed in Model IV did not result in attributing a significant proportion of the variation in anomie to any of the independent variables, although the effect estimates were in the direction predicted. Table 25 evaluates this model.

The deviations indicate that only among owners who do not participate and who are dissatisfied with their neighborhood do we find a large deviation. The observed proportion is .488. The theoretical proportion is .594. Thus a smaller proportion of subclass P (1) is anomic than expected. When sex is introduced as a control variable, however, we do find a relatively strong relationship among females. Among females, 12.6 percent of the variation in feelings of anomie is explained by tenure. Inspection of the data also shows that it is females who have the largest deviations from the theoretical expectancy. In sum, the model provides a good fit for the data even though only about 10 percent of the variation is explained by the independent criterion. Thus, the contention that anomie is relatively high among populations such as the one analyzed in this study is supported.

TABLE 25

Comparison of Theoretical and Observed Proportions
for Model IV

Variable Configuration	Observed Proportions	Theoretical Proportions	Deviation
P (123)	.54	.53	.01
P (12)	.68	.58	.10
P (13)	.50	.54	-.04
P (1)	.49	.59	-.10
P (23)	.50	.58	-.08
P (2)	.61	.63	-.02
P (3)	.66	.59	.07
P*	.63	.64	-.01

SUMMARY

This chapter appraised the relationship between tenure and housing quality. Five theoretical proportions were subjected to an empirical test, and four were found to be tenable. A multivariate analysis was then attempted and the effects of the independent criterion on social adjustment were determined. Finally, an evaluation of the models was presented. A more comprehensive statement of the findings and implications of this research is given in Chapter 6.

NOTES

1. Charles M. Grigg and Lewis Killian, Preliminary Report of Housing Survey, Jacksonville, Florida (Institute for Social Research, Florida State University, 1963).

2. The data used in the construction of Tables 6 and 7 are given in Appendix B.

3. See Appendix B for frequency distribution of social adjustment scores.

The social effects of housing on the individual and his normative orientation to society are complex and dynamic phenomena. This is especially true in a social system changing as rapidly as American society. More important, however, is the changing status of the black American, the unit of analysis in this research. Thus, the complexity of the problem is compounded by the fact that the black Americans in this study are poor, uneducated, and have spent a major portion of their lives in the ghetto of a southern metropolitan area.

With these considerations in mind, this research established four major objectives: (1) To assess the social effects of housing and tenure on the individual's social adjustment by comparing a group of black Americans who were displaced and moved from the slum area to the status of homeowner in a newly developed suburb to a group of black Americans who were displaced to adjacent slums and retained the status of renter; (2) to assess the relationship between social participation and social adjustment; (3) to assess the relationship between neighborhood satisfaction and social adjustment; and (4) to perform a multivariate analysis of the interrelationship between tenure, social participation, neighborhood satisfaction, and social adjustment. The sociological relevance of these objectives was discussed in the review of relevant literature.

In the review, several conceptual statements were derived: (1) Most individuals are goal directed; however, their inability to achieve desirable goals or an uncertainty of suitable methods to use to achieve desired goals often causes problems of orientation for individuals in a specified social system. (2) In urban America, the slum areas of the city represent the end of the line for a large portion of the population; the crucial element here is that the inhabitants of slum areas feel this way about themselves. (3) A change from slum dwelling to suburban living results in a more positive orientation to society.

These general assumptions led to the development of five theoretical propositions to which this research was addressed:

1. There is a positive relationship between tenure and social adjustment.

2. Change in tenure is related to the degree of social participation.

3. Tenure is related to the degree of neighborhood satisfaction.

4. Social participation is related to social adjustment.

5. Neighborhood satisfaction is related to social adjustment.

The major theoretical concepts used in this research were social adjustment, social participation, and neighborhood satisfaction. Social adjustment was assumed to be multidimensional. The dimensions delineated in this research were anomie, social isolation, and powerlessness. Scales were designed to measure the main concepts.

In order to empirically test these propositions, a random sample of 439 was selected from a population of 1700. The 1700 in the original population were black Americans who formerly lived in the most deteriorated section of a large southern metropolitan area.

In the analysis, this research investigated the simple relationships described above and multivariate relationships between tenure, social participation, neighborhood satisfaction, and social adjustment. Also included in the analysis was multivariate analysis of the dimensions of social adjustment. These dimensions included anomie, powerlessness, and isolation.

SUMMARY OF FINDINGS

In the analysis of simple relationships between the change in tenure and quality of housing, the homeowners invariably were more satisfied with their new dwellings. In this phase of the analysis, eight subjective measures of housing quality were analyzed. These measures are (1) satisfaction with heating and cooling equipment; (2) amount of street noise; (3) amount of air and sunlight; (4) amount of open space around the house; (5) amount of room; (6) attitude toward new residence; (7) amount of closet space; and (8) amount of privacy.

The second phase of the analysis was concerned with the relationships between the independent variables and social adjustment. Table 26 summarizes the findings.

TABLE 26

Summary of Simple Variable Relationships

Variable	Nature of Relationships
Tenure	A statistically significant relationship was found between tenure and social adjustment—a higher proportion of homeowners scored high on the social adjustment index. The relationship was moderate as measured by Cramer's V.
Social Participation	A statistically significant relationship was observed between social participation and social adjustment. Individuals frequently participating in voluntary associations scored high on social adjustment. The relationship was not as strong as anticipated.
Neighborhood Satisfaction	The relationship between neighborhood satisfaction and social adjustment was not statistically significant.
Tenure	A statistically significant relationship was found between tenure and social participation. A higher proportion of homeowners participated in voluntary associations than did renters.
Tenure	A statistically significant relationship was found between tenure and neighborhood satisfaction. A higher proportion of homeowners indicated satisfaction. The degree of association was very low.

Following the analysis of simple relationships, a multivariate analysis was attempted. The model employed yields an estimate of the effects of the independent variables on the dependent variable. Table 27 summarizes these findings.

The analysis shows that tenure explains a significant proportion of the variation in social adjustment and powerlessness, while social participation explains a significant proportion of the variation in powerlessness. Neighborhood satisfaction explains a significant proportion of the variation in social adjustment and powerlessness.

CONCLUSIONS

The findings of this study lead to the following conclusions:

1. The slums in metropolitan areas provide the background setting for producing alienated or socially unadjusted individuals. This is especially true for the black population.

2. A move from the slum areas to areas with better quality housing results in a more positive orientation to society.

3. If the move involves a change in tenure from renter to home owner, a significant change in attitude occurs. The feeling of powerlessness is significantly reduced. This is especially true for the black male.

TABLE 27

Summary of Multivariate Analysis of the Effects of Independent Variables on the Dependent Variables.

Independent Variables	Dependent Variables			
	Social Adjustment	Powerlessness	Social Isolation	Anomie
Tenure	.20[a]	.12[a]	.07	.05
Social Participation	-.05	-.13[a]	.08	.01
Neighborhood Satisfaction	-.15[a]	-.11[a]	-.05	.05

[a]Statistical Significance $\underline{Pr} < .02$

4. Although not conclusively demonstrated, the change in tenure results in more frequent participation in community affairs and a greater satisfaction with one's neighborhood.

IMPLICATIONS

The implications of this research are divided into three major types. Each type is discussed below.

Theoretical Implications

There are several theoretical implications derived from this research. One of the most important is that it can provide a basis for the formulation of more specific hypotheses focusing on the social effects of housing and home ownership. Such hypotheses may be advanced to provide some explanations for the social and cultural conditions within the inner city that produce alienated individuals.

This research has demonstrated that there is a need for further theoretical clarification of the concept of social adjustment. Also, there is a need for a more elaborate conceptualization of the dimensions of social adjustment. These dimensions include further elaboration on anomie, powerlessness, and social isolation. Equally important is the use of behavioral items as indicators of social adjustment.

Finally, theoretical consideration should be given the black male. This group obviously is the most alienated in society. In this study, the opportunity to become a homeowner had a significant effect on the black male's sense of powerlessness. Here the research would be interested in identifying other aspects of the social and cultural environment that could act as positive deterrents to alienation.

Methodological Implications

Since it was necessary to construct several scales in the analysis of the data, it is conceivable that more precise measures could be developed. Also, for a study concerned with the problem of attitude change, it would be much more desirable to have had before-after measures on each group. As it turned out, it was necessary to assume that the respondents were relatively homogeneous in their orientation to society. Although the analysis of social and economic characteristics showed only slight deviations, the basic assumptions are subject to question. For example, the motivations that led to buying a home could also be influential in determining social adjustment.

A possible alternative analytical strategy could have been used. A dummy regression model is appropriate for attribute data and would have allowed the inclusion of more variables in a given model. The Coleman's model that was used requires a larger sample because of the dichotomous nature of the subclasses needed when additional variables are introduced.

Finally, there is no limit to the number of independent variables that may be introduced. This research selected variables that are grounded in sociological theory.

Pragmatic Implications

The implications of this research must be considered in view of the contemporary problems facing urban America. As the theoretical frame suggests, the quality of the home environment bears a definite relationship on the normative orientation of individuals to society. In the slum areas of the metropolis is found the conditions that produce alienated and isolated individuals. Thus, flexible programs on the national, state, and local levels are needed to combat the increasing disorganization arising out of slum areas.

APPENDIXES

INTERVIEW SCHEDULE

1. Personal and Housing Background

    1. Race and Sex
       (Interviewer: Check this)

Negro, Male	1	_____
White, Male	2	_____
Negro, Female	3	_____
White, Female	4	_____

    2. Age _____

    3. Marital Status
       (1) single   _____
       (2) married   _____
       (3) widowed   _____
       (4) divorced   _____
       (5) separated   _____

    4. If married, number of children and age
       (Interviewer: If respondent is single, do not ask this
                     question.)
       (1) none   _____
       (2) under 6 years old   _____
       (3) 6-13 years old   _____
       (4) 14-17 years old   _____
       (5) 18 years old and over   _____

    5. How many children under 18 live here with you? _____

    6. Are you presently employed? Yes _____ No _____

    7. What is your present work, or what is your usual work
       when you are employed? (Be specific.) _____
       _____

    8. Is your wife (husband) presently employed?
       Yes _____ No _____

    9. What is her (his) present work, or usual work when she
       (he) is employed? (Be specific.) (Interviewer:
       "Housewife" is a legitimate occupation.) _____
       _____

    10. What is your yearly gross income?
        (0) Under $1, 000   _____
        (1) $1, 000 to $1, 999 _____

89

(2) $2,000 to $2,999 _____   (Interviewer:
(3) $3,000 to $3,999 _____   Hand the respon-
(4) $4,000 to $4,999 _____   dent the WHITE
(5) $5,000 to $5,999 _____   CARD to use in
(6) $6,000 to $6,999 _____   answering this
(7) $7,000 to $7,999 _____   question and
(8) $8,000 to $8,999 _____   questions #11
(9) $9,000 to $9,999 _____   and #12.)
(X) $10,000 to $14,999 _____
(Y) $15,000 and over _____
Don't know _____   No response _____

11. What is your husband's (wife's) yearly gross income?
(0) Under $1,000
(1) $1,000 to $1,999 _____
(2) $2,000 to $2,999 _____
(3) $3,000 to $3,999 _____
(4) $4,000 to $4,999 _____
(5) $5,000 to $5,999 _____
(6) $6,000 to $6,999 _____
(7) $7,000 to $7,999 _____
(8) $8,000 to $8,999 _____
(9) $9,000 to $9,999 _____
(X) $10,000 to $14,999 _____
(Y) $15,000 and over _____
Don't know _____   No response _____

12. What is your total family yearly gross income?
(0) Under $1,000
(1) $1,000 to $1,999 _____
(2) $2,000 to $2,999 _____
(3) $3,000 to $3,999 _____
(4) $4,000 to $4,999 _____
(5) $5,000 to $5,999 _____
(6) $6,000 to $6,999 _____
(7) $7,000 to $7,999 _____
(8) $8,000 to $8,999 _____
(9) $9,000 to $9,999 _____
(X) $10,000 to $14,999 _____
(Y) $15,000 and over _____
Don't know _____   No response _____

13. What is your family's major source of income?
(1) Inherited savings and investments
(2) Investments from earned wealth _____
(3) Profits, fees, royalties _____
(4) Salary, commissions, regular income
     paid on monthly or yearly basis _____

(5) Wages on hourly basis or checks received
weekly   _____

(6) Income from "odd jobs" or private relief
work, "sharecropping" or seasonal work   _____

(7) Public relief or charity   _____

(8) Pensions and social security   _____

(9) Other (specify)   _____

14. How many grades of school have you completed?_____

15. How many grades of school has your husband
(wife) completed?   _____

16. How many grades did your parents complete?
(1) Father _____
(2) Mother _____

17. If you had to tell someone where you lived in Jacksonville, what would you say? (Do not give street address.) _____

_____

18. Do you own this home?
(1) Own   _____
(2) Rent   _____
(3) Other (Specify) _____
(4) No answer   _____

19. How long have you lived in this house?   _____

20. Where in Jacksonville did you live before moving here?
(Street and Number) _____

_____

21. Did you own or rent your former dwelling?
(1) Own   _____
(2) Rent   _____
(3) Other (Specify) _____
(4) No answer   _____

22. How many people live in your house (apartment)? _____

23. How do you feel about the place you live now as compared
with your former residence?
(1) It is much better _____
(2) A little better   _____
(3) About the same   _____

(4) A little worse _____
(5) Much worse _____

24. How many times have you moved since living in Jacksonville? _____

25. If there were no housing shortage, would you like to stay on here or would you like to move from this place?
(1) Stay _____
(2) Move _____

26. Are you very anxious to stay here (move out), or doesn't it matter too much to you?
(1) Anxious _____
(2) Doesn't matter _____

27. Why do you want to stay (move)? _____
_____

28. Now, about this place, by and large, would you say you were satisfied with, dissatisfied with, or doesn't it matter to you about:

	Satisfied	Dissatisfied	Indifferent
(1) Amount of room	1	2	3
(2) Amount of privacy	1	2	3
(3) Amount of closet space	1	2	3
(4) Heating (cooling equipment	1	2	3
(5) Street noises	1	2	3
(6) Rent, maintenance and care expenses	1	2	3
(7) Amount of air and sunlight	1	2	3
(8) Amount of open space around the house	1	2	3

29. How about the location of this house (apartment)—are you satisfied with, dissatisfied with, or doesn't it matter to you about:

	Satisfied	Dissatisfied	Indifferent
(a) Travel conditions to work	1	2	3
	1	2	3
(b) Schools around here	1	2	3
(c) Kind of people around here	1	2	3

	Satisfied	Dissatisfied	Indifferent
(d) Shopping facilities	1	2	3
(e) Nearness to church	1	2	3
(f) Nearness to friends and relatives	1	2	3

30. Do you or your family own a car? Yes _____ No _____
    What year? _____ Model? _____
    More than one _____

31. Would you prefer to own or rent a place to live?
    (1) Own _____
    (2) Rent _____

32. Why? _____
    _____

33. About how much cash do you think it would take to make a
    down payment on the kind of house you would need for
    your family? _____

34. If you had started buying a house and found you couldn't
    keep up the payments, what would be the best thing to do?
    _____

35. If you were going to move from this address, in what part
    of town would you look for a place to live? _____

11. Migration History

    36. Place of birth _____
        (Interviewer: Indicate city, and state, or foreign country.
                      If respondent was born in Jacksonville,
                      place "YY" in space provided.)

    37. In what year did you move to Jacksonville? _____
        (Interviewer: Indicate last two digits of year, i.e., "59"
                      if moved in 1959. If respondent has always
                      lived in Jacksonville, place "YY" in space
                      provided and skip next two questions.)

    38. Where was the last place you lived before moving to
        Jacksonville? _____

39. Why did you move to Jacksonville? _____
_____

III. Attitudes and Participation (Note to Interviewer: If respondent
is not employed, go on to question #42.)

40. About how long have you been at your present job? _____

41. Are you satisfied with your present job?
    (1) Very satisfied   _____
    (2) Satisfied   _____
    (3) Dissatisfied   _____
    (4) Very dissatisfied   _____

42. How many jobs have you held in the past five years?
    _____

43. If you had a choice, what kind of work would you most like
    to do? (Be specific) _____

44. What do you feel are the main things that keep you from
    having the kind of job that you would most like to have?
    _____

45. If you had a chance to do the kind of work you want to
    here in Jacksonville, would you change jobs or employ-
    ment status?
    (1) Yes   _____
    (2) No   _____
    (3) Don't know   _____
    (4) Under certain conditions (specify)_____

    (5) No answer   _____

46. If you had a chance to do this kind of work in another com-
    munity, would you move?
    (1) Yes   _____
    (2) No   _____
    (3) Maybe   _____
    (4) Don't know   _____
    (5) Under certain conditions (specify)   _____
    _____

47. If you have held other jobs, do you enjoy your present
    job more, less than, or about the same as the last one?
    (1) More enjoyable   _____
    (2) Less enjoyable   _____

(3) About the same _____
(4) First job _____

48. It has been said that people in the South feel differently about labor unions than people in other parts of the country. How do you feel about labor unions? _____
_____

49. Would you like your children to have a college education?
(1) Yes _____
(2) No _____
(3) Other (specify)_____
(4) No answer _____

50. Suppose you had two children, one boy and one girl, both of the same age, mental ability, etc. If you could send only one to college, which one would you send and why?
_____
_____

51. What do you think is the main value of a college education? (Interviewer: Ask this question only of Negro respondents. Hand the respondent the Card for question #51 to use in answering.)
(1) To help people get a higher standard of living

(2) To make them better able to deal with other Negroes

(3) To give them an opportunity to do things for others

(4) To gain status and prestige _____
(5) To make them better able to deal with white people

(6) Other (specify) _____

52. What do you think are the chances for boys to find work in Jacksonville when they leave school? If they have had:
(a) an elementary school education (through the 8th grade)
(b) a high school education (through the 12th grade)
(c) a college education
(Interviewer: Hand the respondent the Card to use in answering questions #52 and #53.)

	Elementary	High School	College
(1) Very favorable			
(2) Favorable			
(3) Unfavorable			
(4) Very unfavorable			

96   BLACK HOME OWNERSHIP

53. What do you think the chances for <u>girls</u> to find work in
Jacksonville when they leave school are? If they have had:
(a) an elementary school education (through the 8th grade)
(b) a high school education (through the 12th grade)
(c) a college education

	Elementary	High School	College
(1) Very favorable			
(2) Favorable			
(3) Unfavorable			
(4) Very unfavorable			

54. In general, is it more important for a boy or a girl to be
able to support a family someday? Why?

_____

_____

55. Do you feel this is how it should be? Yes _____ No _____
Why? _____

56. How do you feel about the recreational facilities such as
parks, playgrounds, and swimming pools?
(1) Very satisfied _____
(2) Satisfied _____
(3) Dissatisfied _____
(4) Very dissatisfied _____
Why? _____

_____

57. How do you feel about police protection and services?
(1) Very satisfied _____
(2) Satisfied _____
(3) Dissatisfied _____
(4) Very dissatisfied _____
Why? _____

_____

58. How do you feel about the opportunities to find good housing
in this community?
(1) Very satisfied _____
(2) Satisfied _____
(3) Dissatisfied _____
(4) Very dissatisfied _____
Why? _____

_____

59. What do you feel are the three best things about Jackson-
    ville as a place to live?
    1. _____
    2. _____
    3. _____

60. What do you feel are the three greatest needs of Jackson-
    ville as a community?
    1. _____
    2. _____
    3. _____

61. In your present situation, if you inherited a large sum of
    money, what would be the first three things you would use
    it for?
    1. _____
    2. _____
    3. _____

62. How much do you think each of the following groups is
    doing things in Jacksonville that are in the best interest
    of people like you? (Interviewer: Use Card)

	A Lot	Some	Little	None	Don't Know
(1) White churches	1	2	3	4	5
(2) Negro churches	1	2	3	4	5
(3) Democratic party	1	2	3	4	5
(4) Urban League	1	2	3	4	5
(5) City government	1	2	3	4	5
(6) Republican party	1	2	3	4	5
(7) NAACP	1	2	3	4	5
(8) State government	1	2	3	4	5
(9) CORE	1	2	3	4	5
(10) Chamber of Commerce	1	2	3	4	5
(11) Black Muslims	1	2	3	4	5
(12) Federal government	1	2	3	4	5

		A Lot	Some	Little	None	Don't Know
(13)	Council on Human Relations	1	2	3	4	5
(14)	Labor unions	1	2	3	4	5
(15)	White businessmen	1	2	3	4	5
(16)	Negro businessmen	1	2	3	4	5

63. Now here are some statements that we want you to listen to and then tell us whether you agree or disagree with the statement.

		A	D	Undec.
(1)	Most people don't really care what happens to the next fellow.	1	2	3
(2)	You sometimes can't help wondering whether anything is worthwhile any more.	1	2	3
(3)	Next to health, money is the most important thing in life.	1	2	3
(4)	No one really understands me.	1	2	3
(5)	To make money, there are no right and wrong ways any more, only easy and hard ways.	1	2	3
(6)	I worry about the future facing today's children.	1	2	3
(7)	Sometimes I have the feeling other people are using me.	1	2	3
(8)	There is little or nothing I can do towards preventing a major shooting war.	1	2	3
(9)	There are so many decisions that have to be made today that sometimes I could just blow up.	1	2	3
(10)	It is frightening to be responsible for the development of a little child.	1	2	3
(11)	There is little chance for promotion on the job unless a man gets a break.	1	2	3
(12)	We're so regimented today that there's not much room for choice even in personal matters.	1	2	3
(13)	We are just so many cogs in the machinery of life.	1	2	3
(14)	The future looks very dismal.	1	2	3
(15)	Sometimes I feel all alone in the world.	1	2	3

	A	D	Undec.
(16) I don't get invited out by friends as often as I'd really like.	1	2	3
(17) Most people today seldom feel lonely.	1	2	3
(18) Real friends are as easy as ever to find.	1	2	3
(19) One can always find friends if he shows himself friendly.	1	2	3
(20) The world in which we live is basically a friendly place.	1	2	3
(21) There are few dependable ties between people anymore.	1	2	3
(22) People are just naturally friendly and helpful.	1	2	3
(23) I don't get to visit friends as often as I'd really like.	1	2	3
(24) Religion is mainly a myth.	1	2	3
(25) I think single life is better than married life.	1	2	3
(26) Human life is an expression of divine purpose.	1	2	3

64. Would you please tell me about the organizations of which you are a member?

Name of Organi- zation	Attendance (times per month)	Financial Contributions ($ given yearly)	Member of Com- mittee (yes-no)	Office held (titles)
1.				
2.				
3.				
4.				
5.				
6.				
7.				
8.				

65. In general, among the families you know, is the husband or the wife the real head of the family?
   (1) Husband   _____
   (2) Wife   _____
   (3) They are equal _____
   (4) Don't know   _____

66. Is this the way you think it should be?
   Yes _____ No _____
   Why? _____
   _____

67. What are the things you do most often in your spare time?

_____
_____
_____

68. What are the things you would like to do in your spare time if you had the opportunity?

_____
_____
_____

69. Do you suppose you will ever have the opportunity to do these things?
    (1) Yes _____
    (2) No _____
    Why? _____
    _____

70. In your family, is it (was it) generally the husband or the wife who makes the decisions about:

	Husband	Wife	Both
(1) How the money is spent.	1	2	3
(2) Disciplining the children.	1	2	3
(3) Family recreation.	1	2	3
(4) The children's education—what schools are attended and how long.	1	2	3

71. Inventory of facilities; (Interviewer: Mark those categories that apply.)

	Present Dwelling	Previous Dwelling
(a) What type of water facilities do you have in the house?		
1. Running water inside (cold only)	_____	_____
2. Running water inside (cold and hot)	_____	_____
3. Running outside	_____	_____
4. Hand pump outside	_____	_____
5. Hand pump inside		
Y. Other	_____	_____
X. No answer	_____	_____

	Present Dwelling	Previous Dwelling
(b) Kind of bathing facilities		
0. None	_____	_____
1. Tub	_____	_____
2. Shower	_____	_____
3. Tub and shower	_____	_____
4. Portable tub only	_____	_____
Y. Other	_____	_____
X. No answer	_____	_____
(c) Do you have electricity?		
0. None	_____	_____
1. Electricity	_____	_____
2. Kerosene (or gas)	_____	_____
Y. Other (specify)	_____	_____
(d) Do you have a refrigerator?		
0. None	_____	_____
1. Electric or gas	_____	_____
2. Ice box	_____	_____
Y. Other (specify)	_____	_____
X. No answer	_____	_____
(e) Does the household have a radio and television?		
0. None (neither radio nor television)	_____	_____
1. Radio	_____	_____
2. Television	_____	_____
3. Radio and television	_____	_____
X. No answer	_____	_____
(f) Is there a telephone in the house?		
0. None	_____	_____
1. Private line	_____	_____

<u>Present Dwelling Previous Dwelling</u>

2. Party line
Y. Other (specify)
X. No answer

TABLE A. 1

Frequency Distribution of Social Adjustment Scores

Social Adjustment Score	Frequency	Percent
26-30	7	1.59
31-35	97	22.10
36-40	165	37.59
41-45	134	30.52
46-52	36	8.20
Total	439	100.00

TABLE A. 2

Relationship between Tenure and Attitude
Toward Amount of Air and Sunlight

	Owner		Renter	
	Number	Percent	Number	Percent
Satisfied	308	96.25	116	86.56
Dissatisfied	12	3.75	18	13.44
Total	320	100.00	134	100.00
$x^2 = 14.42$		$\underline{Pr} < .0005$		$\underline{V} = .18$

TABLE A.3

Relationship between Tenure and Attitude
Toward Street Noises

	Owner		Renter	
	Number	Percent	Number	Percent
Satisfied	282	88.40	104	77.03
Dissatisfied	37	11.60	31	22.97
Total	319	100.00	135	100.00
$x^2 = 9.62$		Pr$<$ .005		V $=$ .15

TABLE A.4

Relationship between Tenure and Attitude
Toward Heating (Cooling) Equipment

	Owner		Renter	
	Number	Percent	Number	Percent
Satisfied	240	75.70	81	61.36
Dissatisfied	77	24.30	51	38.64
Total	317	100.00	132	100.00
$x^2 = 9.41$		Pr$<$ .005		V $=$ .15

TABLE A. 5

Relationship between Tenure and Attitude
Toward Amount of Room

	Owner		Renter	
	Number	Percent	Number	Percent
Satisfied	262	81.61	82	60.74
Dissatisfied	59	18.39	53	39.26
Total	321	100.00	135	100.00

x^2 = 22.36 $\qquad$ $\underline{Pr} < .0005$ $\qquad$ $\underline{V}$ = .22

TABLE A. 6

Relationship between Tenure and Attitude
Toward Amount of Open Space Around the House

	Owner		Renter	
	Number	Percent	Number	Percent
Satisfied	307	96.84	91	73.98
Dissatisfied	10	3.16	32	26.02
Total	317	100.00	123	100.00

x^2 = 53.64 $\qquad$ $\underline{Pr} < .0005$ $\qquad$ $\underline{V}$ = .35

TABLE A. 7

Relationship between Tenure and Attitude
Toward Amount of Privacy

	Owner		Renter	
	Number	Percent	Number	Percent
Satisfied	293	91.27	96	71.11
Dissatisfied	28	8.73	39	28.89
Total	321	100.00	135	100.00
x^2 = 30.83		$\underline{Pr} < .0005$		$\underline{V}$ = .26

TABLE A. 8

Relationship between Tenure and Attitude
Toward Amount of Closet Space

	Owner		Renter	
	Number	Percent	Number	Percent
Satisfied	256	80.50	66	48.52
Dissatisfied	62	19.50	70	51.48
Total	318	100.00	136	100.00
x^2 = 47.23		$\underline{Pr} < .0005$		$\underline{V}$ = .32

TABLE A. 9

Relationship between Tenure and Attitude
Toward New Residence

	Owner		Renter	
	Number	Percent	Number	Percent
Satisfied (Better)	304	94.70	94	69.11
Dissatisfied (Worse)	17	5.30	42	30.89
Total	321	100.00	136	100.00
$x^2 = 55.62$	Pr $<$ .0005		V = .35	

109

TABLE A.10

Relation of Tenure, Social Participation, and
Neighborhood Satisfaction to Low Social
Adjustment

| | Owner | | | | Renter | | | |
| | Participant | | Nonparticipant | | Participant | | Nonparticipant | |
	Satisfied	Dissatisfied	Satisfied	Dissatisfied	Satisfied	Dissatisfied	Satisfied	Dissatisfied
	22	41	27	31	7	9	19	35
N	54	102	68	84	8	23	32	68
Pi	.41	.40	.40	.37	.87	.39	.59	.51
P^*	.49	.34	.44	.29	.69	.54	.64	.49
$Pi-P^*$	-.08	.06	-.04	.08	.18	-.15	-.05	.02

a_1 = Effect of neighborhood satisfaction = -.15
a_2 = Effect of social participation = -.05
a_3 = Effect of tenure = .20

r = .49
s = .51

z_1 = -2.73 pr = .0032
z_2 = -.92 pr = .1788
z_3 = 3.65 pr = .000135

Pi = Observed proportion
P^* = Theoretical proportion
$Pi-P^*$ = Deviation

110

TABLE A.11

Relation of Tenure, Social Participation, and Neighborhood Satisfaction to High Powerlessness

	Owner				Renter			
	Participant		Nonparticipant		Participant		Nonparticipant	
	Satisfied	Dissatisfied	Satisfied	Dissatisfied	Satisfied	Dissatisfied	Satisfied	Dissatisfied
	22	48	26	29	7	8	13	31
N	54	102	68	84	8	23	32	68
Pi	.41	.47	.38	.35	.88	.35	.41	.46
P^*	.51	.39	.38	.27	.63	.51	.50	.39
$Pi-P^*$	-.10	.08	.08	.08	.25	-.16	-.09	.07

a_1 = Effect of neighborhood satisfaction = -.11
a_2 = Effect of social participation = -.13
a_3 = Effect of tenure = .12

r = .51
s = .61

z_1 = -2.06 pr = .0197
z_2 = -2.34 pr = .0096
z_3 = 2.19 pr = .0143

Pi = Observed proportion
P^* = Theoretical proportion
$Pi-P^*$ = Deviation

111

TABLE A.12

Relation of Tenure, Social Participation, and Neighborhood Satisfaction to High Social Isolation

	Owner				Renter			
	Participant		Nonparticipant		Participant		Nonparticipant	
	Satisfied	Dissatisfied	Satisfied	Dissatisfied	Satisfied	Dissatisfied	Satisfied	Dissatisfied
	35	52	31	49	4	12	27	42
N	54	102	68	84	8	23	32	68
Pi	.65	.51	.46	.58	.50	.52	.84	.62
$P*$	.54	.48	.62	.56	.61	.55	.69	-.63
$Pi-P*$	.11	.03	-.16	.02	-.11	-.03	.15	-.01

a_1 = Effect of neighborhood satisfaction = -.05
a_2 = Effect of social participation = .08
a_3 = Effect of tenure = .07

r = .54
s = .36

z_1 = -.86 pr = .1949
z_2 = 1.29 pr = .0985
z_3 = 1.15 pr = .1251

Pi = Observed proportion
$P*$ = Theoretical proportion
$Pi-P*$ = Deviation

TABLE A. 13

Relation of Tenure, Social Participation, and Neighborhood Satisfaction to High Anomie

| | Owner | | | | Renter | | | |
| | Participant | | Nonparticipant | | Participant | | Nonparticipant | |
	Satisfied	Dissatisfied	Satisfied	Dissatisfied	Satisfied	Dissatisfied	Satisfied	Dissatisfied
	29	69	34	41	4	14	21	43
N	54	102	68	84	8	23	32	68
Pi	.54	.68	.50	.49	.50	.61	.66	.63
$P*$	.53	.58	.54	.59	.58	.63	.59	.64
$Pi-P*$	.01	.10	-.04	-.10	-.08	-.02	.07	-.01

a_1 = Effect of neighborhood satisfaction = .05
a_2 = Effect of social participation = .01
a_3 = Effect of tenure = .05

r = .53
s = .36

z_1 = .83 pr = .20
z_2 = .18 pr = .43
z_3 = .71 pr = .24

Pi = Observed proportion
$P*$ = Theoretical proportion
$Pi-P*$ = Deviation

TABLE A.14

Relation of Tenure, Social Participation, and Neighborhood Satisfaction to Low Social Adjustment among Females

	Owner				Renter			
	Participant		Nonparticipant		Participant		Nonparticipant	
	Satisfied	Dissatisfied	Satisfied	Dissatisfied	Satisfied	Dissatisfied	Satisfied	Dissatisfied
	12	26	18	15	3	7	13	14
N	31	59	32	39	4	13	16	27
Pi	.39	.44	.56	.38	.75	.54	.81	.52
P^*	.50	.34	.54	.38	.71	.56	.75	.60
$Pi-P^*$	-.11	.10	.02	0	.04	-.02	.06	-.08

a_1 = Effect of neighborhood satisfaction = -.16
a_2 = Effect of social participation = .04
a_3 = Effect of tenure = .21

r = .50
s = .41

z_1 = 1.90 pr = .0287
z_2 = .49 pr = .3121
z_3 = 2.54 pr = .0055

Pi = Observed proportion
P^* = Theoretical proportion
$Pi-P^*$ = Deviation

114

TABLE A.15

Relation of Tenure, Social Participation, and Neighborhood Satisfaction to Low Social Adjustment among Males

	Owner				Renter			
	Participant		Nonparticipant		Participant		Nonparticipant	
	Satisfied	Dissatisfied	Satisfied	Dissatisfied	Satisfied	Dissatisfied	Satisfied	Dissatisfied
	10	15	9	16	4	2	6	21
N	23	43	36	45	4	10	16	41
P_i	.43	.35	.25	.36	1.00	.20	.38	.51
P^*	.49	.33	.35	.19	.66	.50	.52	.36
P_i-P^*	-.06	.02	-.10	.17	.34	-.30	-.14	.15

a_1 = Effect of neighborhood satisfaction = -.16
a_2 = Effect of social participation = -.14
a_3 = Effect of tenure = .17

r = .49
s = .64

z_1 = -2.40 pr = .0082
z_2 = -2.12 pr = .0170
z_3 = 2.60 pr = .0047

P_i = Observed proportion
P^* = Theoretical proportion
P_i-P^* = Deviation

TABLE A.16

Relation of Tenure, Social Participation, and Neighborhood
Satisfaction to High Powerlessness among Females

| | Owner | | | | Renter | | | |
| | Participant | | Nonparticipant | | Participant | | Nonparticipant | |
	Satisfied	Dissatisfied	Satisfied	Dissatisfied	Satisfied	Dissatisfied	Satisfied	Dissatisfied
	13	31	14	12	3	7	6	8
N	31	59	32	39	4	13	16	27
Pi	.42	.53	.44	.31	.75	.54	.38	.30
P^*	.56	.49	.36	.28	.63	.55	.43	.35
$Pi-P^*$	-.14	.04	.08	.03	.12	-.01	-.05	-.05

a_1 = Effect of neighborhood satisfaction = -.08
a_2 = Effect of social participation = -.20
a_3 = Effect of tenure = .07

r = .56
s = .65

z_1 = -.93   pr = .1762
z_2 = -2.43   pr = .0075
z_3 = .80   pr = .2119

Pi = Observed proportion
P^* = Theoretical proportion
$Pi-P^*$ = Deviation

116

TABLE A.17

Relation of Tenure, Social Participation, and Neighborhood Satisfaction to High Powerlessness among Males

	Owner				Renter			
	Participant		Nonparticipant		Participant		Nonparticipant	
	Satisfied	Dissatisfied	Satisfied	Dissatisfied	Satisfied	Dissatisfied	Satisfied	Dissatisfied
	9	17	12	17	4	1	7	23
N	23	43	36	45	4	10	16	41
Pi	.39	.40	.33	.38	1.00	.10	.44	.56
P^*	.49	.31	.44	.26	.64	.46	.59	.41
$Pi-P^*$	-.10	.09	-.11	.12	.36	-.36	-.15	.15

a_1 = Effect of neighborhood satisfaction = -.18
a_2 = Effect of social participation = -.04
a_3 = Effect of tenure = .15
r = .49
s = .58

z_1 = -3.03 pr = .0012
z_2 = -.74 pr = .2296
z_3 = 2.50 pr = .0062

Pi = Observed proportion
P^* = Theoretical proportion
$Pi-P^*$ = Deviation

TABLE A.18

Relation of Tenure, Social Participation, and Neighborhood
Satisfaction to High Social Isolation among Females

| | Owner | | | | Renter | | | |
| | Participant | | Nonparticipant | | Participant | | Nonparticipant | |
	Satisfied	Dissatisfied	Satisfied	Dissatisfied	Satisfied	Dissatisfied	Satisfied	Dissatisfied
	22	30	16	21	1	7	12	14
N	31	59	32	39	4	13	16	27
Pi	.71	.51	.50	.54	.25	.54	.75	.52
$P*$	.54	.51	.62	.59	.49	.46	.57	.54
$Pi-P*$	.17	0	-.12	-.05	-.24	.08	.18	-.02

a_1 = Effect of neighborhood satisfaction = -.03
a_2 = Effect of social participation = .08
a_3 = Effect of tenure = -.05

r = .54
s = .46

pr = .3745
pr = .1841
pr = .2743

z_1 = .32
z_2 = .90
z_3 = .60

Pi = Observed proportion
P* = Theoretical proportion
Pi-P* = Deviation

118

TABLE A.19

Relation of Tenure, Social Participation, and Neighborhood Satisfaction to High Social Isolation among Males

	Owner				Renter			
	Participant		Nonparticipant		Participant		Nonparticipant	
	Satisfied	Dissatisfied	Satisfied	Dissatisfied	Satisfied	Dissatisfied	Satisfied	Dissatisfied
	13	22	15	28	3	5	15	28
$\underline{N}$	23	43	36	45	4	10	16	41
$\underline{Pi}$	.57	.51	.42	.62	.75	.50	.94	.68
$\underline{P^*}$	.53	.44	.61	.53	.72	.63	.80	.71
$\underline{Pi-P^*}$	.04	.07	-.19	.09	.03	-.13	.14	-.03

a_1 = Effect of neighborhood satisfaction = -.09
a_2 = Effect of social participation = .08
a_3 = Effect of tenure = .19

$\underline{r}$ = .5315
$\underline{s}$ = .29

z_1 = -1.07 $\underline{pr}$ = .1423
z_2 = 1.01 $\underline{pr}$ = .1562
z_3 = 2.29 $\underline{pr}$ = .0110

Pi = Observed proportion
$\overline{P^*}$ = Theoretical proportion
$\overline{Pi-P^*}$ = Deviation

119

TABLE A. 20

Relation of Tenure, Social Participation, and Neighborhood Satisfaction to High Anomie among Females

| | Owner | | | | Renter | | | |
| | Participant | | Nonparticipant | | Participant | | Nonparticipant | |
	Satisfied	Dissatisfied	Satisfied	Dissatisfied	Satisfied	Dissatisfied	Satisfied	Dissatisfied
	15	41	18	22	2	10	14	18
N	31	59	32	39	4	13	16	27
Pi	.48	.69	.56	.56	.50	.77	.88	.67
P^*	.51	.58	.57	.64	.64	.71	.70	.76
$Pi-P^*$	-.03	.11	-.01	-.08	-.14	.06	.18	-.09

a_1 = Effect of neighborhood satisfaction = .07
a_2 = Effect of social participation = .06
a_3 = Effect of tenure = .13

r = .51
s = .23

pr = .2119
pr = .2578
pr = .0694

z_1 = .80
z_2 = .65
z_3 = 1.48

Pi = Observed proportion
P^* = Theoretical proportion
$Pi-P^*$ = Deviation

TABLE A. 21

Relation of Tenure, Social Participation, and Neighborhood
Satisfaction to High Anomie among Males

	Owner				Renter			
	Participant		Nonparticipant		Participant		Nonparticipant	
	Satisfied	Dissatisfied	Satisfied	Dissatisfied	Satisfied	Dissatisfied	Satisfied	Dissatisfied
	14	28	16	19	2	4	7	25
N	23	43	36	45	4	10	16	41
Pi	.61	.65	.44	.42	.50	.40	.44	.61
$P*$	.55	.57	.49	.51	.51	.53	.44	.47
$Pi-P*$	.06	.08	-.05	-.09	-.01	-.13	0	.14

a_1 = Effect of neighborhood satisfaction = .02
a_2 = Effect of social participation = -.06
a_3 = Effect of tenure = -.04

r = .55
s = .53

pr = .4013
pr = .2514
pr = .3121

z_1 = .25
z_2 = -.67
z_3 = -.49

Pi = Observed proportion
$P*$ = Theoretical proportion
$Pi-P*$ = Deviation

SELECTED BIBLIOGRAPHY

BOOKS

Abrams, Charles. Man's Struggle for Shelter in an Urbanizing World. Cambridge, Massachusetts: The M.I.T. Press, 1964.

Back, Kurt W. Slums, Projects, and People. Durham, N. C.: Duke University Press, 1962.

Besag, Frank P. Alienation and Education, An Empirical Approach. Buffalo, N.Y.: Hertillon Press, 1966.

Blalock, H. M., Jr. Social Statistics. New York: McGraw-Hill Book Company, 1960.

Boskoff, Alvin. The Sociology of Urban Regions. New York: Meredith Publishing Company, 1962.

Chinoy, Ely. Automobile Workers and the American Dream. Boston: Beacon Press, 1965.

Clinard, Marshall B., ed. Anomie and Deviant Behavior: A Discussion and Critique. New York: The Free Press of Glencoe, 1964.

Cohen, Arthur R. Attitude Change and Social Influence. New York: Basic Books, Inc., 1964.

Coleman, James S. Introduction to Mathematical Sociology. Glencoe, Ill.: The Free Press, 1964.

DeGrazia, Sebastian. The Political Community: A Study of Anomie. Chicago: University of Chicago Press, 1948.

Durkheim, Emile. The Division of Labor in Society. Translated by George Simpson. New York: The Macmillan Co., 1933.

_____. Suicide. Translated by John A. Spaulding and George Simpson. New York: The Free Press, 1951.

Festinger, Leon; Schachter, Stanley; and Back, Kurt W. Social Pressures in Informal Groups: A Study of Human Factors in Housing. New York: Harper & Brothers, 1950.

Frazier, E. Franklin. The Negro Family in Chicago. Chicago: University of Chicago Press, 1932.

Fromm, Eric. The Sane Society. New York: Holt, Rinehart and Winston, Inc., 1955.

Gans, Herbert J. "Effects of the Move from City to Suburb." The
Urban Condition. Edited by Leonard J. Duhl. New York:
Basic Books, Inc., 1963.

Glazer, Nathan, and McEntire, D. Studies in Housing and Minority
Groups. Berkeley: University of California Press, 1960.

Guttman, Louis. Measurement and Prediction. Studies in Social
Psychology in World War II, edited by Samuel Stouffer, et al.,
vol. IV. Princeton: Princeton University Press, 1950.

Hilgard, Ernest R. Introduction to Psychology. New York: Harcourt,
Brace & World, 1962.

Hunter, David R. The Slums: Challenge and Response. New York:
The Free Press, 1964.

Lander, Bernard. Toward an Understanding of Juvenile Delinquency.
New York: Columbia University Press, 1954.

Laurenti, Luigi. Property Values and Race: Studies in Seven Cities.
Berkeley: University of California Press, 1960.

McCord, William, et al. Life Styles in the Black Ghetto. New York:
W. W. Norton and Company, 1969.

Meltzer, Jack. "Relocation of Families Displaced in Urban Redevelopment: Experience in Chicago." Urban Redevelopment: Problems and
Practices. Edited by Coleman Woodbury. Chicago: University
of Chicago Press, 1953.   •

Merton, Robert K. "The Social Psychology of Housing." Current
Trends in Social Psychology. Edited by Wayne Dennis. Pittsburgh: University of Pittsburgh Press, 1951.

_____. Social Theory and Social Structure. Glencoe, Ill.: The
Free Press, 1957.

Mizruchi, Ephraim Harold. Success and Opportunity: A Study of
Anomie. New York: The Free Press, 1964.

Reid, M. G. Housing and Income. Chicago: University of Chicago
Press, 1962.

Selltiz, Claire, et al. Research Methods in Social Relations. New
York: Holt, Rinehart and Winston, 1964.

Spinley, B. M. The Deprived and the Privileged. New York: Humanities Press, 1953.

Warner, Lloyd, and Srole, Leo. The Social Systems of American Ethnic Groups. New Haven: Yale University Press, 1945.

Williams, Robin. American Society. New York: Alfred A. Knopf, Inc., 1950.

Wilner, Daniel M., et al. The Housing Environment and Family Life. Baltimore: The Johns Hopkins Press, 1962.

Woodbury, Coleman, ed. The Future of Cities and Urban Redevelopment. Chicago: University of Chicago Press, 1953.

_____. Urban Redevelopment: Problems and Practices. Chicago: University of Chicago Press, 1953.

ARTICLES

Barrington, Moore, Jr. "Sociological Theory and Contemporary Politics," American Journal of Sociology, LXI (September, 1955), 107-115.

Bauer, Catherine. "Social Questions in Housing and Community Planning," Journal of Social Issues, VII, 1 (1951), 1-34.

Becker, Howard. "Normative Reactions to Normlessness," American Sociological Review, XXV (December, 1960), 803-810.

Browning, Charles J., et al. "On the Meaning of Alienation," American Sociological Review, XXVI (October, 1961), 780-781.

Brunsman, Howard G. "Current Sources of Sociological Data in Housing," American Sociological Review, XII (April, 1947), 150-155.

Butler, E. W., et al. "Demographic and Social Psychological Factors in Residential Mobility," Sociology and Social Research, XLVIII (January, 1964), 139-154.

Caplow, Theodore. "Home Ownership and Location Preferences in a Minneapolis Sample," American Sociological Review, XIII (December, 1948), 725-730.

128   BLACK HOME OWNERSHIP

Carpenter, Niles. "Attitude Patterns in the Home-Buying Family,"
Social Forces, XI (October, 1932), 76-81.

Catton, William R., Jr. "A Theory of Value," American Sociological
Review, XXIV (June, 1959), 310-317.

Chapin, F. S. "An Experiment on the Social Effects of Good Housing,"
American Sociological Review, V (December, 1940), 868-879.

_____. "A Study of Social Adjustment Using the Technique of
Analysis by Selective Control," Social Forces, XVIII (May,
1940), 476-487.

_____. "New Methods of Sociological Research on Housing Prob-
lems," American Sociological Review, XII (April, 1947), 143-
149.

_____. "Some Housing Factors Related to Mental Hygiene,"
Journal of Social Issues, VII, 2 (1951), 164-171.

Cohen, Albert K. "The Sociology of the Deviant Act: Anomie Theory
and Beyond," American Sociological Review, XXX (February,
1965), 5-14.

Dean, Dwight G. "Alienation: Its Meaning and Measurement," American Sociological Review, XXVI (October, 1961), 753-758.

Dean, John P. "The Ghosts of Home Ownership," Journal of Social
Issues, VII, 1 (1951), 59-68.

Dubin, Robert. "Deviant Behavior and Social Structure: Continuities
in Social Theory," American Sociological Review, XXIV (April,
1959), 147-164.

Elais, Gabriel. "The Concept and an Objective Measure of Homelessness," Studies in Higher Education, LXXVII (August, 1951).

Festinger, Leon. "Architecture and Group Membership," Journal
of Social Issues, VII, 2 (1951), 152-163.

Form, William H. "Stratification in Low and Middle Income Housing
Areas," Journal of Social Issues, VII, 2 (1951), 109-131.

Goode, William J. "Illegitimacy, Anomie, and Cultural Penetration,"
American Sociological Review, XXVI (December, 1961), 910-
925.

Gullahorn John T., and Gullahorn, Jeanne E. "A Computer Model
    of Elementary Social Behavior," Behavioral Science, VIII
    (October, 1963), 354-362.

Guttman, Louis. "A Basis for Scaling Qualitative Data," American
    Sociological Review, IX (April, 1944), 139-150.

Guttman, Louis. "The Cornell Technique for Scale and Intensity
    Analysis," Educational and Psychological Measurement, VII
    (Summer, 1947), 247-280.

Harlan, Howard, and Wherry, Jack. "Delinquency and Housing,"
    Social Forces, XXVII (October, 1948), 58-61.

Hartman, Chester W. "Social Values and Housing Orientations,"
    Journal of Social Issues, XIX (April, 1963), 113-131.

Hole, Vere. "Social Effects of Planned Rehousing," Town Planning
    Review, XXX (July, 1959).

Horton, John. "The Dehumanization of Anomie and Alienation: A
    Problem in the Ideology of Sociology," British Journal of So-
    ciology, XV (1964), 283-300.

Jones, Clifton R. "Invasion and Racial Attitudes: A Study of Housing
    in a Border City," Social Forces, XXVII (March, 1949), 285-290.

Kochen, Manfred. "The Logical Nature of an Action Scheme," Behav-
    ioral Science, I (October, 1956), 265-289.

Kohn, Melvin L., and John A. Clausen. "Social Isolation and Schi-
    zophrenia," American Sociological Review, XX (June, 1955),
    265-272.

Lefton, Mark. "Race, Expectations and Anomie," Social Forces,
    XLVI (March, 1968), 347-352.

Leevy, J. Roy. "Contrasts in Urban and Rural Family Life," Ameri-
    can Sociological Review, V (December, 1940), 948-953.

Loring, William C. "Housing Characteristics and Social Disorgani-
    zation," Social Problems, III (January, 1956).

Lowry, Ritchie P. "The Functions of Alienation in Leadership,"
    Sociology and Social Research, XLVI (July, 1962), 426-435.

McClosky, Herbert, and Schaar, John H. "Psychological Dimensions of Anomie," American Sociological Review, XXX (February, 1965), 14-40.

Meier, Dorothy, and Bell, Wendell. "Anomia and Differential Access to the Achievement of Life Goals," American Sociological Review, XXIV (April, 1959), 189-202.

Miller, Curtis R., and Butler, Edgar W. "Anomie and Eunomia: A Methodological Evaluation of Srole's Anomie Scale," American Sociological Review, XXXI (June, 1966), 400-406.

Miller James. "Toward a Unified Theory of Human Behavior," Behavioral Science, I (October, 1956), 319-326.

Millspaugh, Martin. "Problems and Opportunities of Relocation," Law and Contemporary Problems, XXVI (Winter, 1961), 6-36.

Mizruchi, Ephraim Harold. "Social Structure and Anomie in a Small City," American Sociological Review, XXV (October, 1960), 645-654.

Mogey, J. M. "Changes in Family Life Experienced by English Workers Moving from Slums to Housing Estates," Marriage and Family Living, XVII (May, 1955), 123-128.

Montgomery, D. S. "Relocation and Its Impact on Families," Social Casework, XLI (October, 1960), 402-407.

Morris, Richard T., and Jeffries, Vincent. "Violence Next Door," Social Forces, XLVI (March, 1968), 352-358.

Munch, Peter A. "Social Adjustment Among Wisconsin Norwegians," American Sociological Review, XIV (December, 1949), 780-787.

Neal, Arthur G., and Rettig, Salomon. "On the Multidimensionality of Alienation," American Sociological Review, XXXII (February, 1967), 54-64.

Nettler, Gwynn. "A Measure of Alienation," American Sociological Review, XXII (December, 1957), 670-677.

Plutchik, Robert. "Operationalism as Methodology," Behavioral Science, VIII (July, 1963), 234-241.

Reimer, Svend. "Architecture for Family Living," Journal of Social Issues, VII, 2 (1951), 140-151.

_____. "Sociological Theory of Home Adjustment, " American
Sociological Review, VIII (June, 1943), 272-278.

Reynolds, Harry W. "What Do We Know About Our Experiences with
Relocation?" Journal of Intergroup Relations, II (Autumn, 1961),
342-354.

Rosow, Irving. "Home Ownership Motives, " American Sociological
Review, XIII (December, 1948), 751-756.

Scott, William A. "Empirical Assessment of Values and Ideologies, "
American Sociological Review, XXIV (June, 1959), 299-310.

Seeman, Melvin. "On the Meaning of Alienation, " American Sociological Review, XXIV (December, 1959), 783-791.

Simpson, Richard L. "A Note on Status, Mobility, and Anomie, "
British Journal of Sociology, XI (December, 1960), 370-372.

Srole, Leo. "Social Integration and Certain Corollaries: An Exploratory Study, " American Sociological Review, XXI (December,
1956), 709-716.

Starbuck, William. "Level of Aspiration Theory and Economic Behavior, " Behavioral Science, VIII (April, 1963), 128-136.

Turner, Ralph. "Value-Conflict in Social Disorganization, " Sociology
and Social Research, XXXVIII (May, 1954), 301-308.

Wilson, James Q. "The War on Cities, " The Public Interest, III
(Spring, 1966), 31-32.

Wirth, Louis. "Housing as a Field of Sociological Research, "
American Sociological Review, XII (April, 1947), 137-143.

_____. "Urbanism as a Way of Life, " American Journal of Sociol-
ogy, XLIV (July, 1938), 1-24.

Works, Ernest. "Residence in Integrated and Segregated Housing
and Improvement in Self-Concepts of Negroes, " Sociology and
Social Research, XLVI (April, 1962), 294-301.

MISCELLANEOUS MATERIAL

Cagle, Lawrence T. , and Deutscher, Irwin. "Housing Aspirations
of Low-Income Fatherless Families. " Mimeographed paper,

Syracuse, N. Y.: Syracuse University Youth Development
Center, n. d.

Coons, Alvin E., and Glaze, Bert T. "Housing Market Analysis and
the Growth of Nonfarm Home Ownership." Bureau of Business
Research Monograph Number 115. Columbus: Ohio State University, 1963.

Cottam, H. R. "Housing and Attitudes Toward Housing in Rural
Pennsylvania." Bulletin 436. University Park, Pennsylvania:
School of Agriculture, Pennsylvania State College.

Goldstein, Sidney, and Zimmer, Basil G. "Residential Displacement
and Resettlement of the Aged: A Study of Problems of Rehousing
Aged Residents Displaced by Freeway Construction in Downtown
Providence." Providence: Rhode Island Division on Aging, 1960

Grigg, Charles M., and Killian, Lewis M. "Preliminary Report of
Housing Survey, Jacksonville, Florida." Tallahassee: Institute
for Social Research, Florida State University, 1963.

Hanson, Robert, and Graves, Theodore D. "Objective Access, Anomie
and Deviance in a Tri-Ethnic Community." Paper presented at
the meeting of the American Sociological Association, Los Angeles, August, 1963.

Sewell, William H. The Construction and Standardization of a Scale
for the Measurement of the Socio-Economic Status of Oklahoma
Farm Families. Stillwater, Pennsylvania, Oklahoma A & M
Agricultural Experiment Station Technical Bulletin No. 9. April,
1940.

U.S. Senate, Subcommittee of the Committee on Banking and Currenrency. Study of Mortgage Credit. 86th Congress, 1st Session.
Washington, D. C.: Government Printing Office, 1959.

U. S., Statutes at Large. LXIII, Part 1, 413-445.

Watts, Lewis G., et al. "The Middle-Income Negro Family Faces
Urban Renewal." Research Center of the Florence Heller
Graduate School for Advanced Studies in Social Welfare, Brandeis University 1964.

ABOUT THE AUTHOR

WILLIAM A. STACEY is Assistant Professor in the Department of Sociology, University of Texas at Arlington. Professor Stacey re received his Master of Arts degree in sociology and educational psychology from Mississippi State University in 1961 and obtained his doctorate at Florida State University in 1965. Before joining the faculty of the University of Texas, Professor Stacey held the position of Assistant Professor of Sociology at Mississippi State University, where he divided his time equally between teaching and research.

E   Stacey, William A
185.89   Black home owner-
H6   ship
S7

    DEC 18   S H 3 4 5 4